Buddhist Ethics: A Very Short Introduction

VERY SHORT INTRODUCTIONS are for anyone wanting a stimulating and accessible way into a new subject. They are written by experts, and have been translated into more than 45 different languages.

The series began in 1995, and now covers a wide variety of topics in every discipline. The VSI library currently contains over 650 volumes—a Very Short Introduction to everything from Psychology and Philosophy of Science to American History and Relativity—and continues to grow in every subject area.

Very Short Introductions available now:

ABOLITIONISM Richard S. Newman
THE ABRAHAMIC RELIGIONS
    Charles L. Cohen
ACCOUNTING Christopher Nobes
ADAM SMITH Christopher J. Berry
ADOLESCENCE Peter K. Smith
ADVERTISING Winston Fletcher
AERIAL WARFARE Frank Ledwidge
AESTHETICS Bence Nanay
AFRICAN AMERICAN RELIGION
    Eddie S. Glaude Jr
AFRICAN HISTORY John Parker and
    Richard Rathbone
AFRICAN POLITICS Ian Taylor
AFRICAN RELIGIONS
    Jacob K. Olupona
AGEING Nancy A. Pachana
AGNOSTICISM Robin Le Poidevin
AGRICULTURE Paul Brassley and
    Richard Soffe
ALBERT CAMUS Oliver Gloag
ALEXANDER THE GREAT
    Hugh Bowden
ALGEBRA Peter M. Higgins
AMERICAN CULTURAL HISTORY
    Eric Avila
AMERICAN FOREIGN RELATIONS
    Andrew Preston
AMERICAN HISTORY Paul S. Boyer
AMERICAN IMMIGRATION
    David A. Gerber
AMERICAN LEGAL HISTORY
    G. Edward White
AMERICAN NAVAL HISTORY
    Craig L. Symonds

AMERICAN POLITICAL HISTORY
    Donald Critchlow
AMERICAN POLITICAL PARTIES
    AND ELECTIONS L. Sandy Maisel
AMERICAN POLITICS
    Richard M. Valelly
THE AMERICAN PRESIDENCY
    Charles O. Jones
THE AMERICAN REVOLUTION
    Robert J. Allison
AMERICAN SLAVERY
    Heather Andrea Williams
THE AMERICAN WEST
    Stephen Aron
AMERICAN WOMEN'S HISTORY
    Susan Ware
ANAESTHESIA Aidan O'Donnell
ANALYTIC PHILOSOPHY
    Michael Beaney
ANARCHISM Colin Ward
ANCIENT ASSYRIA Karen Radner
ANCIENT EGYPT Ian Shaw
ANCIENT EGYPTIAN ART AND
    ARCHITECTURE Christina Riggs
ANCIENT GREECE Paul Cartledge
THE ANCIENT NEAR EAST
    Amanda H. Podany
ANCIENT PHILOSOPHY Julia Annas
ANCIENT WARFARE
    Harry Sidebottom
ANGELS David Albert Jones
ANGLICANISM Mark Chapman
THE ANGLO-SAXON AGE John Blair
ANIMAL BEHAVIOUR
    Tristram D. Wyatt

THE ANIMAL KINGDOM
    Peter Holland
ANIMAL RIGHTS David DeGrazia
THE ANTARCTIC Klaus Dodds
ANTHROPOCENE Erle C. Ellis
ANTISEMITISM Steven Beller
ANXIETY Daniel Freeman and
    Jason Freeman
THE APOCRYPHAL GOSPELS
    Paul Foster
APPLIED MATHEMATICS
    Alain Goriely
ARCHAEOLOGY Paul Bahn
ARCHITECTURE Andrew Ballantyne
ARISTOCRACY William Doyle
ARISTOTLE Jonathan Barnes
ART HISTORY Dana Arnold
ART THEORY Cynthia Freeland
ARTIFICIAL INTELLIGENCE
    Margaret A. Boden
ASIAN AMERICAN HISTORY
    Madeline Y. Hsu
ASTROBIOLOGY David C. Catling
ASTROPHYSICS James Binney
ATHEISM Julian Baggini
THE ATMOSPHERE Paul I. Palmer
AUGUSTINE Henry Chadwick
AUSTRALIA Kenneth Morgan
AUTISM Uta Frith
AUTOBIOGRAPHY Laura Marcus
THE AVANT GARDE David Cottington
THE AZTECS David Carrasco
BABYLONIA Trevor Bryce
BACTERIA Sebastian G. B. Amyes
BANKING John Goddard and
    John O. S. Wilson
BARTHES Jonathan Culler
THE BEATS David Sterritt
BEAUTY Roger Scruton
BEHAVIOURAL ECONOMICS
    Michelle Baddeley
BESTSELLERS John Sutherland
THE BIBLE John Riches
BIBLICAL ARCHAEOLOGY
    Eric H. Cline
BIG DATA Dawn E. Holmes
BIOGRAPHY Hermione Lee
BIOMETRICS Michael Fairhurst
BLACK HOLES Katherine Blundell
BLOOD Chris Cooper
THE BLUES Elijah Wald

THE BODY Chris Shilling
THE BOOK OF COMMON PRAYER
    Brian Cummings
THE BOOK OF MORMON
    Terryl Givens
BORDERS Alexander C. Diener and
    Joshua Hagen
THE BRAIN Michael O'Shea
BRANDING Robert Jones
THE BRICS Andrew F. Cooper
THE BRITISH CONSTITUTION
    Martin Loughlin
THE BRITISH EMPIRE Ashley Jackson
BRITISH POLITICS Anthony Wright
BUDDHA Michael Carrithers
BUDDHISM Damien Keown
BUDDHIST ETHICS Damien Keown
BYZANTIUM Peter Sarris
C. S. LEWIS James Como
CALVINISM Jon Balserak
CANCER Nicholas James
CAPITALISM James Fulcher
CATHOLICISM Gerald O'Collins
CAUSATION Stephen Mumford and
    Rani Lill Anjum
THE CELL Terence Allen and
    Graham Cowling
THE CELTS Barry Cunliffe
CHAOS Leonard Smith
CHARLES DICKENS Jenny Hartley
CHEMISTRY Peter Atkins
CHILD PSYCHOLOGY Usha Goswami
CHILDREN'S LITERATURE
    Kimberley Reynolds
CHINESE LITERATURE Sabina Knight
CHOICE THEORY Michael Allingham
CHRISTIAN ART Beth Williamson
CHRISTIAN ETHICS D. Stephen Long
CHRISTIANITY Linda Woodhead
CIRCADIAN RHYTHMS
    Russell Foster and Leon Kreitzman
CITIZENSHIP Richard Bellamy
CIVIL ENGINEERING
    David Muir Wood
CLASSICAL LITERATURE William Allan
CLASSICAL MYTHOLOGY
    Helen Morales
CLASSICS Mary Beard and
    John Henderson
CLAUSEWITZ Michael Howard
CLIMATE Mark Maslin

CLIMATE CHANGE Mark Maslin
CLINICAL PSYCHOLOGY
    Susan Llewelyn and
    Katie Aafjes-van Doorn
COGNITIVE NEUROSCIENCE
    Richard Passingham
THE COLD WAR Robert McMahon
COLONIAL AMERICA Alan Taylor
COLONIAL LATIN AMERICAN
    LITERATURE Rolena Adorno
COMBINATORICS Robin Wilson
COMEDY Matthew Bevis
COMMUNISM Leslie Holmes
COMPARATIVE LITERATURE
    Ben Hutchinson
COMPLEXITY John H. Holland
THE COMPUTER Darrel Ince
COMPUTER SCIENCE
    Subrata Dasgupta
CONCENTRATION CAMPS
    Dan Stone
CONFUCIANISM Daniel K. Gardner
THE CONQUISTADORS
    Matthew Restall and
    Felipe Fernández-Armesto
CONSCIENCE Paul Strohm
CONSCIOUSNESS Susan Blackmore
CONTEMPORARY ART
    Julian Stallabrass
CONTEMPORARY FICTION
    Robert Eaglestone
CONTINENTAL PHILOSOPHY
    Simon Critchley
COPERNICUS Owen Gingerich
CORAL REEFS Charles Sheppard
CORPORATE SOCIAL
    RESPONSIBILITY Jeremy Moon
CORRUPTION Leslie Holmes
COSMOLOGY Peter Coles
COUNTRY MUSIC Richard Carlin
CRIME FICTION Richard Bradford
CRIMINAL JUSTICE Julian V. Roberts
CRIMINOLOGY Tim Newburn
CRITICAL THEORY
    Stephen Eric Bronner
THE CRUSADES Christopher Tyerman
CRYPTOGRAPHY Fred Piper and
    Sean Murphy
CRYSTALLOGRAPHY A. M. Glazer
THE CULTURAL REVOLUTION
    Richard Curt Kraus

DADA AND SURREALISM
    David Hopkins
DANTE Peter Hainsworth and
    David Robey
DARWIN Jonathan Howard
THE DEAD SEA SCROLLS
    Timothy H. Lim
DECADENCE David Weir
DECOLONIZATION Dane Kennedy
DEMOCRACY Bernard Crick
DEMOGRAPHY Sarah Harper
DEPRESSION Jan Scott and
    Mary Jane Tacchi
DERRIDA Simon Glendinning
DESCARTES Tom Sorell
DESERTS Nick Middleton
DESIGN John Heskett
DEVELOPMENT Ian Goldin
DEVELOPMENTAL BIOLOGY
    Lewis Wolpert
THE DEVIL Darren Oldridge
DIASPORA Kevin Kenny
DICTIONARIES Lynda Mugglestone
DINOSAURS David Norman
DIPLOMACY Joseph M. Siracusa
DOCUMENTARY FILM
    Patricia Aufderheide
DREAMING J. Allan Hobson
DRUGS Les Iversen
DRUIDS Barry Cunliffe
DYNASTY Jeroen Duindam
DYSLEXIA Margaret J. Snowling
EARLY MUSIC Thomas Forrest Kelly
THE EARTH Martin Redfern
EARTH SYSTEM SCIENCE Tim Lenton
ECONOMICS Partha Dasgupta
EDUCATION Gary Thomas
EGYPTIAN MYTH Geraldine Pinch
EIGHTEENTH-CENTURY BRITAIN
    Paul Langford
THE ELEMENTS Philip Ball
EMOTION Dylan Evans
EMPIRE Stephen Howe
ENERGY SYSTEMS Nick Jenkins
ENGELS Terrell Carver
ENGINEERING David Blockley
THE ENGLISH LANGUAGE
    Simon Horobin
ENGLISH LITERATURE Jonathan Bate
THE ENLIGHTENMENT
    John Robertson

ENTREPRENEURSHIP Paul Westhead
    and Mike Wright
ENVIRONMENTAL ECONOMICS
    Stephen Smith
ENVIRONMENTAL ETHICS
    Robin Attfield
ENVIRONMENTAL LAW
    Elizabeth Fisher
ENVIRONMENTAL POLITICS
    Andrew Dobson
EPICUREANISM Catherine Wilson
EPIDEMIOLOGY Rodolfo Saracci
ETHICS Simon Blackburn
ETHNOMUSICOLOGY Timothy Rice
THE ETRUSCANS Christopher Smith
EUGENICS Philippa Levine
THE EUROPEAN UNION
    Simon Usherwood and John Pinder
EUROPEAN UNION LAW
    Anthony Arnull
EVOLUTION Brian and
    Deborah Charlesworth
EXISTENTIALISM Thomas Flynn
EXPLORATION Stewart A. Weaver
EXTINCTION Paul B. Wignall
THE EYE Michael Land
FAIRY TALE Marina Warner
FAMILY LAW Jonathan Herring
FASCISM Kevin Passmore
FASHION Rebecca Arnold
FEDERALISM Mark J. Rozell and
    Clyde Wilcox
FEMINISM Margaret Walters
FILM Michael Wood
FILM MUSIC Kathryn Kalinak
FILM NOIR James Naremore
THE FIRST WORLD WAR
    Michael Howard
FOLK MUSIC Mark Slobin
FOOD John Krebs
FORENSIC PSYCHOLOGY
    David Canter
FORENSIC SCIENCE Jim Fraser
FORESTS Jaboury Ghazoul
FOSSILS Keith Thomson
FOUCAULT Gary Gutting
THE FOUNDING FATHERS
    R. B. Bernstein
FRACTALS Kenneth Falconer
FREE SPEECH Nigel Warburton
FREE WILL Thomas Pink

FREEMASONRY Andreas Önnerfors
FRENCH LITERATURE John D. Lyons
THE FRENCH REVOLUTION
    William Doyle
FREUD Anthony Storr
FUNDAMENTALISM Malise Ruthven
FUNGI Nicholas P. Money
THE FUTURE Jennifer M. Gidley
GALAXIES John Gribbin
GALILEO Stillman Drake
GAME THEORY Ken Binmore
GANDHI Bhikhu Parekh
GARDEN HISTORY Gordon Campbell
GENES Jonathan Slack
GENIUS Andrew Robinson
GENOMICS John Archibald
GEOFFREY CHAUCER David Wallace
GEOGRAPHY John Matthews and
    David Herbert
GEOLOGY Jan Zalasiewicz
GEOPHYSICS William Lowrie
GEOPOLITICS Klaus Dodds
GERMAN LITERATURE Nicholas Boyle
GERMAN PHILOSOPHY
    Andrew Bowie
GLACIATION David J. A. Evans
GLOBAL CATASTROPHES Bill McGuire
GLOBAL ECONOMIC
    HISTORY Robert C. Allen
GLOBALIZATION Manfred Steger
GOD John Bowker
GOETHE Ritchie Robertson
THE GOTHIC Nick Groom
GOVERNANCE Mark Bevir
GRAVITY Timothy Clifton
THE GREAT DEPRESSION AND THE
    NEW DEAL Eric Rauchway
HABERMAS James Gordon Finlayson
THE HABSBURG EMPIRE
    Martyn Rady
HAPPINESS Daniel M. Haybron
THE HARLEM RENAISSANCE
    Cheryl A. Wall
THE HEBREW BIBLE AS LITERATURE
    Tod Linafelt
HEGEL Peter Singer
HEIDEGGER Michael Inwood
THE HELLENISTIC AGE
    Peter Thonemann
HEREDITY John Waller
HERMENEUTICS Jens Zimmermann

HERODOTUS Jennifer T. Roberts
HIEROGLYPHS Penelope Wilson
HINDUISM Kim Knott
HISTORY John H. Arnold
THE HISTORY OF ASTRONOMY
    Michael Hoskin
THE HISTORY OF
    CHEMISTRY William H. Brock
THE HISTORY OF CHILDHOOD
    James Marten
THE HISTORY OF CINEMA
    Geoffrey Nowell-Smith
THE HISTORY OF LIFE
    Michael Benton
THE HISTORY OF MATHEMATICS
    Jacqueline Stedall
THE HISTORY OF MEDICINE
    William Bynum
THE HISTORY OF PHYSICS
    J. L. Heilbron
THE HISTORY OF TIME
    Leofranc Holford-Strevens
HIV AND AIDS Alan Whiteside
HOBBES Richard Tuck
HOLLYWOOD Peter Decherney
THE HOLY ROMAN EMPIRE
    Joachim Whaley
HOME Michael Allen Fox
HOMER Barbara Graziosi
HORMONES Martin Luck
HUMAN ANATOMY
    Leslie Klenerman
HUMAN EVOLUTION Bernard Wood
HUMAN RIGHTS Andrew Clapham
HUMANISM Stephen Law
HUME A. J. Ayer
HUMOUR Noël Carroll
THE ICE AGE Jamie Woodward
IDENTITY Florian Coulmas
IDEOLOGY Michael Freeden
THE IMMUNE SYSTEM
    Paul Klenerman
INDIAN CINEMA
    Ashish Rajadhyaksha
INDIAN PHILOSOPHY Sue Hamilton
THE INDUSTRIAL REVOLUTION
    Robert C. Allen
INFECTIOUS DISEASE Marta L. Wayne
    and Benjamin M. Bolker
INFINITY Ian Stewart
INFORMATION Luciano Floridi
INNOVATION Mark Dodgson and
    David Gann
INTELLECTUAL PROPERTY
    Siva Vaidhyanathan
INTELLIGENCE Ian J. Deary
INTERNATIONAL LAW Vaughan Lowe
INTERNATIONAL MIGRATION
    Khalid Koser
INTERNATIONAL RELATIONS
    Christian Reus-Smit
INTERNATIONAL SECURITY
    Christopher S. Browning
IRAN Ali M. Ansari
ISLAM Malise Ruthven
ISLAMIC HISTORY Adam Silverstein
ISOTOPES Rob Ellam
ITALIAN LITERATURE
    Peter Hainsworth and David Robey
JESUS Richard Bauckham
JEWISH HISTORY David N. Myers
JOURNALISM Ian Hargreaves
JUDAISM Norman Solomon
JUNG Anthony Stevens
KABBALAH Joseph Dan
KAFKA Ritchie Robertson
KANT Roger Scruton
KEYNES Robert Skidelsky
KIERKEGAARD Patrick Gardiner
KNOWLEDGE Jennifer Nagel
THE KORAN Michael Cook
KOREA Michael J. Seth
LAKES Warwick F. Vincent
LANDSCAPE ARCHITECTURE
    Ian H. Thompson
LANDSCAPES AND
    GEOMORPHOLOGY
    Andrew Goudie and Heather Viles
LANGUAGES Stephen R. Anderson
LATE ANTIQUITY Gillian Clark
LAW Raymond Wacks
THE LAWS OF THERMODYNAMICS
    Peter Atkins
LEADERSHIP Keith Grint
LEARNING Mark Haselgrove
LEIBNIZ Maria Rosa Antognazza
LEO TOLSTOY Liza Knapp
LIBERALISM Michael Freeden
LIGHT Ian Walmsley
LINCOLN Allen C. Guelzo

LINGUISTICS Peter Matthews
LITERARY THEORY Jonathan Culler
LOCKE John Dunn
LOGIC Graham Priest
LOVE Ronald de Sousa
MACHIAVELLI Quentin Skinner
MADNESS Andrew Scull
MAGIC Owen Davies
MAGNA CARTA Nicholas Vincent
MAGNETISM Stephen Blundell
MALTHUS Donald Winch
MAMMALS T. S. Kemp
MANAGEMENT John Hendry
MAO Delia Davin
MARINE BIOLOGY Philip V. Mladenov
THE MARQUIS DE SADE John Phillips
MARTIN LUTHER Scott H. Hendrix
MARTYRDOM Jolyon Mitchell
MARX Peter Singer
MATERIALS Christopher Hall
MATHEMATICAL FINANCE
    Mark H. A. Davis
MATHEMATICS Timothy Gowers
MATTER Geoff Cottrell
THE MEANING OF LIFE
    Terry Eagleton
MEASUREMENT David Hand
MEDICAL ETHICS Michael Dunn and
    Tony Hope
MEDICAL LAW Charles Foster
MEDIEVAL BRITAIN John Gillingham
    and Ralph A. Griffiths
MEDIEVAL LITERATURE
    Elaine Treharne
MEDIEVAL PHILOSOPHY
    John Marenbon
MEMORY Jonathan K. Foster
METAPHYSICS Stephen Mumford
METHODISM William J. Abraham
THE MEXICAN REVOLUTION
    Alan Knight
MICHAEL FARADAY
    Frank A. J. L. James
MICROBIOLOGY Nicholas P. Money
MICROECONOMICS Avinash Dixit
MICROSCOPY Terence Allen
THE MIDDLE AGES Miri Rubin
MILITARY JUSTICE Eugene R. Fidell
MILITARY STRATEGY
    Antulio J. Echevarria II

MINERALS David Vaughan
MIRACLES Yujin Nagasawa
MODERN ARCHITECTURE
    Adam Sharr
MODERN ART David Cottington
MODERN CHINA Rana Mitter
MODERN DRAMA
    Kirsten E. Shepherd-Barr
MODERN FRANCE
    Vanessa R. Schwartz
MODERN INDIA Craig Jeffrey
MODERN IRELAND Senia Pašeta
MODERN ITALY Anna Cento Bull
MODERN JAPAN
    Christopher Goto-Jones
MODERN LATIN AMERICAN
    LITERATURE
    Roberto González Echevarría
MODERN WAR Richard English
MODERNISM Christopher Butler
MOLECULAR BIOLOGY Aysha Divan
    and Janice A. Royds
MOLECULES Philip Ball
MONASTICISM Stephen J. Davis
THE MONGOLS Morris Rossabi
MOONS David A. Rothery
MORMONISM Richard Lyman Bushman
MOUNTAINS Martin F. Price
MUHAMMAD Jonathan A. C. Brown
MULTICULTURALISM Ali Rattansi
MULTILINGUALISM John C. Maher
MUSIC Nicholas Cook
MYTH Robert A. Segal
NAPOLEON David Bell
THE NAPOLEONIC WARS
    Mike Rapport
NATIONALISM Steven Grosby
NATIVE AMERICAN LITERATURE
    Sean Teuton
NAVIGATION Jim Bennett
NAZI GERMANY Jane Caplan
NELSON MANDELA Elleke Boehmer
NEOLIBERALISM Manfred Steger and
    Ravi Roy
NETWORKS Guido Caldarelli and
    Michele Catanzaro
THE NEW TESTAMENT
    Luke Timothy Johnson
THE NEW TESTAMENT AS
    LITERATURE Kyle Keefer

NEWTON Robert Iliffe
NIELS BOHR J. L. Heilbron
NIETZSCHE Michael Tanner
NINETEENTH-CENTURY BRITAIN
    Christopher Harvie and
    H. C. G. Matthew
THE NORMAN CONQUEST
    George Garnett
NORTH AMERICAN INDIANS
    Theda Perdue and Michael D. Green
NORTHERN IRELAND
    Marc Mulholland
NOTHING Frank Close
NUCLEAR PHYSICS Frank Close
NUCLEAR POWER Maxwell Irvine
NUCLEAR WEAPONS
    Joseph M. Siracusa
NUMBER THEORY Robin Wilson
NUMBERS Peter M. Higgins
NUTRITION David A. Bender
OBJECTIVITY Stephen Gaukroger
OCEANS Dorrik Stow
THE OLD TESTAMENT
    Michael D. Coogan
THE ORCHESTRA D. Kern Holoman
ORGANIC CHEMISTRY
    Graham Patrick
ORGANIZATIONS Mary Jo Hatch
ORGANIZED CRIME
    Georgios A. Antonopoulos and
    Georgios Papanicolaou
ORTHODOX CHRISTIANITY
    A. Edward Siecienski
PAGANISM Owen Davies
PAIN Rob Boddice
THE PALESTINIAN-ISRAELI
    CONFLICT Martin Bunton
PANDEMICS Christian W. McMillen
PARTICLE PHYSICS Frank Close
PAUL E. P. Sanders
PEACE Oliver P. Richmond
PENTECOSTALISM William K. Kay
PERCEPTION Brian Rogers
THE PERIODIC TABLE Eric R. Scerri
PHILOSOPHY Edward Craig
PHILOSOPHY IN THE ISLAMIC
    WORLD Peter Adamson
PHILOSOPHY OF BIOLOGY
    Samir Okasha
PHILOSOPHY OF LAW
    Raymond Wacks
PHILOSOPHY OF SCIENCE
    Samir Okasha
PHILOSOPHY OF RELIGION
    Tim Bayne
PHOTOGRAPHY Steve Edwards
PHYSICAL CHEMISTRY Peter Atkins
PHYSICS Sidney Perkowitz
PILGRIMAGE Ian Reader
PLAGUE Paul Slack
PLANETS David A. Rothery
PLANTS Timothy Walker
PLATE TECTONICS Peter Molnar
PLATO Julia Annas
POETRY Bernard O'Donoghue
POLITICAL PHILOSOPHY
    David Miller
POLITICS Kenneth Minogue
POPULISM Cas Mudde and
    Cristóbal Rovira Kaltwasser
POSTCOLONIALISM Robert Young
POSTMODERNISM Christopher Butler
POSTSTRUCTURALISM
    Catherine Belsey
POVERTY Philip N. Jefferson
PREHISTORY Chris Gosden
PRESOCRATIC PHILOSOPHY
    Catherine Osborne
PRIVACY Raymond Wacks
PROBABILITY John Haigh
PROGRESSIVISM Walter Nugent
PROHIBITION W. J. Rorabaugh
PROJECTS Andrew Davies
PROTESTANTISM Mark A. Noll
PSYCHIATRY Tom Burns
PSYCHOANALYSIS Daniel Pick
PSYCHOLOGY Gillian Butler and
    Freda McManus
PSYCHOLOGY OF MUSIC
    Elizabeth Hellmuth Margulis
PSYCHOPATHY Essi Viding
PSYCHOTHERAPY Tom Burns and
    Eva Burns-Lundgren
PUBLIC ADMINISTRATION
    Stella Z. Theodoulou and Ravi K. Roy
PUBLIC HEALTH Virginia Berridge
PURITANISM Francis J. Bremer
THE QUAKERS Pink Dandelion
QUANTUM THEORY
    John Polkinghorne
RACISM Ali Rattansi
RADIOACTIVITY Claudio Tuniz

RASTAFARI Ennis B. Edmonds
READING Belinda Jack
THE REAGAN REVOLUTION Gil Troy
REALITY Jan Westerhoff
RECONSTRUCTION Allen. C. Guelzo
THE REFORMATION Peter Marshall
RELATIVITY Russell Stannard
RELIGION IN AMERICA Timothy Beal
THE RENAISSANCE Jerry Brotton
RENAISSANCE ART
    Geraldine A. Johnson
RENEWABLE ENERGY Nick Jelley
REPTILES T. S. Kemp
REVOLUTIONS Jack A. Goldstone
RHETORIC Richard Toye
RISK Baruch Fischhoff and John Kadvany
RITUAL Barry Stephenson
RIVERS Nick Middleton
ROBOTICS Alan Winfield
ROCKS Jan Zalasiewicz
ROMAN BRITAIN Peter Salway
THE ROMAN EMPIRE
    Christopher Kelly
THE ROMAN REPUBLIC
    David M. Gwynn
ROMANTICISM Michael Ferber
ROUSSEAU Robert Wokler
RUSSELL A. C. Grayling
RUSSIAN HISTORY Geoffrey Hosking
RUSSIAN LITERATURE Catriona Kelly
THE RUSSIAN REVOLUTION
    S. A. Smith
SAINTS Simon Yarrow
SAVANNAS Peter A. Furley
SCEPTICISM Duncan Pritchard
SCHIZOPHRENIA Chris Frith and
    Eve Johnstone
SCHOPENHAUER
    Christopher Janaway
SCIENCE AND RELIGION
    Thomas Dixon
SCIENCE FICTION David Seed
THE SCIENTIFIC REVOLUTION
    Lawrence M. Principe
SCOTLAND Rab Houston
SECULARISM Andrew Copson
SEXUAL SELECTION Marlene Zuk and
    Leigh W. Simmons
SEXUALITY Véronique Mottier
SHAKESPEARE'S COMEDIES
    Bart van Es

SHAKESPEARE'S SONNETS AND
    POEMS Jonathan F. S. Post
SHAKESPEARE'S TRAGEDIES
    Stanley Wells
SIKHISM Eleanor Nesbitt
THE SILK ROAD James A. Millward
SLANG Jonathon Green
SLEEP Steven W. Lockley and
    Russell G. Foster
SMELL Matthew Cobb
SOCIAL AND CULTURAL
    ANTHROPOLOGY
    John Monaghan and Peter Just
SOCIAL PSYCHOLOGY Richard J. Crisp
SOCIAL WORK Sally Holland and
    Jonathan Scourfield
SOCIALISM Michael Newman
SOCIOLINGUISTICS John Edwards
SOCIOLOGY Steve Bruce
SOCRATES C. C. W. Taylor
SOUND Mike Goldsmith
SOUTHEAST ASIA James R. Rush
THE SOVIET UNION Stephen Lovell
THE SPANISH CIVIL WAR
    Helen Graham
SPANISH LITERATURE Jo Labanyi
SPINOZA Roger Scruton
SPIRITUALITY Philip Sheldrake
SPORT Mike Cronin
STARS Andrew King
STATISTICS David J. Hand
STEM CELLS Jonathan Slack
STOICISM Brad Inwood
STRUCTURAL ENGINEERING
    David Blockley
STUART BRITAIN John Morrill
THE SUN Philip Judge
SUPERCONDUCTIVITY
    Stephen Blundell
SUPERSTITION Stuart Vyse
SYMMETRY Ian Stewart
SYNAESTHESIA Julia Simner
SYNTHETIC BIOLOGY
    Jamie A. Davies
SYSTEMS BIOLOGY Eberhard O. Voit
TAXATION Stephen Smith
TEETH Peter S. Ungar
TELESCOPES Geoff Cottrell
TERRORISM Charles Townshend
THEATRE Marvin Carlson
THEOLOGY David F. Ford

THINKING AND REASONING
 Jonathan St B. T. Evans
THOMAS AQUINAS Fergus Kerr
THOUGHT Tim Bayne
TIBETAN BUDDHISM
 Matthew T. Kapstein
TIDES David George Bowers and
 Emyr Martyn Roberts
TOCQUEVILLE Harvey C. Mansfield
TOPOLOGY Richard Earl
TRAGEDY Adrian Poole
TRANSLATION Matthew Reynolds
THE TREATY OF VERSAILLES
 Michael S. Neiberg
TRIGONOMETRY
 Glen Van Brummelen
THE TROJAN WAR Eric H. Cline
TRUST Katherine Hawley
THE TUDORS John Guy
TWENTIETH-CENTURY BRITAIN
 Kenneth O. Morgan
TYPOGRAPHY Paul Luna
THE UNITED NATIONS
 Jussi M. Hanhimäki
UNIVERSITIES AND COLLEGES
 David Palfreyman and Paul Temple
THE U.S. CONGRESS Donald A. Ritchie
THE U.S. CONSTITUTION
 David J. Bodenhamer

THE U.S. SUPREME COURT
 Linda Greenhouse
UTILITARIANISM
 Katarzyna de Lazari-Radek and
 Peter Singer
UTOPIANISM Lyman Tower Sargent
VETERINARY SCIENCE James Yeates
THE VIKINGS Julian D. Richards
VIRUSES Dorothy H. Crawford
VOLTAIRE Nicholas Cronk
WAR AND TECHNOLOGY
 Alex Roland
WATER John Finney
WAVES Mike Goldsmith
WEATHER Storm Dunlop
THE WELFARE STATE David Garland
WILLIAM SHAKESPEARE
 Stanley Wells
WITCHCRAFT Malcolm Gaskill
WITTGENSTEIN A. C. Grayling
WORK Stephen Fineman
WORLD MUSIC Philip Bohlman
THE WORLD TRADE
 ORGANIZATION Amrita Narlikar
WORLD WAR II
 Gerhard L. Weinberg
WRITING AND SCRIPT
 Andrew Robinson
ZIONISM Michael Stanislawski

Available soon:

FIRE Andrew C. Scott
ECOLOGY Jaboury Ghazoul
MODERN BRAZIL Anthony W. Pereira

BIOGEOGRAPHY
 Mark V. Lomolino
ÉMILE ZOLA Brian Nelson

For more information visit our website

www.oup.com/vsi/

Damien Keown

BUDDHIST ETHICS

A Very Short Introduction

SECOND EDITION

OXFORD
UNIVERSITY PRESS

Great Clarendon Street, Oxford, OX2 6DP,
United Kingdom

Oxford University Press is a department of the University of Oxford.
It furthers the University's objective of excellence in research, scholarship,
and education by publishing worldwide. Oxford is a registered trade mark of
Oxford University Press in the UK and in certain other countries

First edition published 2005
This edition published 2020

Impression: 1

Published in the United States of America by Oxford University Press
198 Madison Avenue, New York, NY 10016, United States of America

British Library Cataloguing in Publication Data
Data available

Library of Congress Control Number: 2019957616

ISBN 978-0-19-885005-2

Printed in Great Britain by
Ashford Colour Press Ltd, Gosport, Hampshire

Contents

Acknowledgements xv

Preface xvii

List of illustrations xxi

Note on citations and pronunciation xxiii

Language and pronunciation xxv

1 Buddhist morality 1

2 Ethics East and West 17

3 Animals and the environment 31

4 Sexuality and gender 48

5 War, violence, and terrorism 61

6 Abortion 77

7 Suicide and euthanasia 93

8 Clones, cyborgs, and singularities 107

Glossary 125

References 127

Further reading 133

Index 141

Buddhist Ethics

Acknowledgements

This book is based on a course taught at Goldsmiths College, London, and I am grateful to present and past students for their interest in the subject and their questions and comments over the years. I am grateful to Goldsmiths College and to the Arts and Humanities Research Board for funding sabbatical leave to allow me to complete the book during the academic year 2003–4, and to the publishers for permission to reuse some material mainly from Chapters 2 and 8 of my companion volume, *Buddhism: A Very Short Introduction*. I am also indebted to my former student Pragati Sahni for her assistance with Chapter 3. Finally, I would like to thank George Miller for inaugurating this project during his time with the Press, and Emma Simmons and Marsha Filion for seeing the first edition of the volume through to publication. My thanks also to Jenny Nugee and Rebecca Darly for their assistance with the second edition. Finally, I am indebted to my literary agent Tony Morris for his help and encouragement at every stage of the way.

Preface

The discipline of Buddhist ethics is a product of the encounter
between two complex and largely independent fields of
knowledge—Buddhism and ethics. Separate introductions to
both are available in the present series, and this short work
makes no attempt to replace them. Instead, it focuses on the
point where these subjects intersect to form a new field of
enquiry, one that has only recently begun to receive the attention
it deserves.

A basic knowledge of Buddhism is assumed in the pages that
follow, and readers who lack this are advised to consult first
my companion volume *Buddhism: A Very Short Introduction*.
Some material relating to ethics there has been adapted for use
here, notably the explanation of karma in Chapter 1, but the
discussion of basic doctrines such as the Four Noble Truths has
not been repeated.

The book is written for a broad general readership. It is intended
for Buddhists interested in ethical questions, for ethicists interested
in Buddhism, for senior school or university students exploring the
ethics of Buddhism (perhaps in conjunction with other world
religions), and for the general reader who is simply curious about
whether an Eastern tradition such as Buddhism can shed any light
on problems that the West has found difficult and divisive.

The reader will find in these pages an overview of how Buddhism might respond to some of the ethical dilemmas confronting the modern world. Six issues of contemporary concern are discussed: animals and the environment; sexuality and gender; war, violence, and terrorism; abortion; suicide and euthanasia; and recent developments in science and technology. As a preliminary to addressing these topics, the first chapter explains the basic moral teachings of Buddhism and the second considers how these teachings might be classified in terms of Western theories of ethics. Since Buddhist ethics is an unfamiliar subject in the West, a strategy adopted in some chapters is to take the more familiar Christian perspective as a point of departure. This allows comparisons and contrasts to be drawn with Buddhism, and hopefully will accelerate the reader's grasp of what is distinctive in the Buddhist approach.

Since this book was first published in 2005 interest in Buddhist ethics has grown considerably. Testimony to this is the publication of the *Oxford Handbook of Buddhist Ethics* (2018), a valuable compendium of research for readers seeking greater depth than is possible in this introduction. Reflecting the growth and sophistication of the discipline, the present volume has been extensively modified. A broader range of theoretical perspectives has been discussed in Chapter 2, and all the chapters have been updated to take into account recent global social and political developments. Chapter 8 has been almost entirely rewritten to take into account the latest scientific advances and the Transhumanist future some believe lies ahead. Since the six issues addressed in the first edition have lost none of their contemporary importance, however, the original selection of topics has been retained.

The 'Buddhism' discussed in the present work is not that of any one school, culture, or historical period, and, although my own expertise is in Theravāda Buddhism, my remarks are made with respect to what for convenience might be termed 'mainstream

Buddhism'. By this I mean the Buddhism taught in authoritative scriptural sources and practised in the Asia-Pacific region which today is home to almost 99 per cent of the world's Buddhists. Socially conservative in nature, this 'mainstream Buddhism' may be contrasted with 'modernist' conceptions of Buddhism found mainly in the West that are generally more liberal in their ethical views, and points of tension between the two will become apparent in the following chapters.

While endeavouring to represent the views of the mainstream, however, this work has no pretensions to being authoritative or definitive. It scarcely needs saying that the issues explored here are controversial, and while some readers may find that the approach taken is congenial to their own reading of Buddhism, others will no doubt disagree, perhaps strongly, with the conclusions reached. Disagreements on ethical matters are almost inevitable given the nature of the subject matter, but hopefully even readers who disagree will feel better informed about alternative perspectives. Overall, I have tried to adopt the role of sympathetic critic, identifying what I see as both the strengths and weaknesses of the Buddhist perspective in the hope of generating a productive dialogue. Readers who wish to pursue the questions discussed at greater length will find guidance in the further reading section at the end.

List of illustrations

1   Map of Buddhism in
    Asia **2**

2   The Bodhisattva
    Avalokiteśvara, the
    embodiment of
    compassion **14**
    Courtesy of John Powers, Deakin
    University.

3   Buddha head in tree roots,
    Wat Mahathat, Ayutthaya,
    Thailand **38**
    © Justin Vidamo 2012
    (CC BY 2.0).

4   The wheel of life **39**

5   Mipham **71**
    Courtesy of Noedup Rongae.

6   Jizō Bosatsu **87**
    Mary Griggs Burke Collection, Gift of
    the Mary and Jackson Burke
    Foundation, 2015.

7   Mizuko Jizō memorial at
    Raikoji (Kamakura,
    Japan) **90**
    Mark Schumacher (www.
    onmarkproductions.com).

8   Suicide of Buddhist monk
    Thich Quang Duc in Saigon,
    1963 **94**
    Granger Historical Picture Archive /
    Alamy Stock Photo.

9   A robot modelled after the
    bodhisattva Kannon
    (Avalokiteśvara) gives its first
    teachings at the Kodaiji
    temple in Kyoto on
    23 February 2019 **116**
    Aflo Co. Ltd. / Alamy Stock Photo |||
    tera.ken/Shutterstock.com.

10 Ray Kurzweil believes the
    Singularity is close at
    hand **117**
    © Ray Kurzweil.

Note on citations and pronunciation

From time to time, the reader will encounter references in the form D. ii.95. These are references to Buddhist scriptures, specifically the Pali Text Society editions of the Theravāda Buddhist canon. This is known as the 'Pali Canon' because the texts are written in the Pali language, a derivative of Sanskrit. The key to the reference is as follows. The initial letter refers to one of the collections (*nikāyas*) into which the Buddha's discourses (*suttas*) are collated.

D Dīgha Nikāya
M Majjhima Nikāya
A Aṅguttara Nikāya
S Saṃyutta Nikāya

The Roman numeral (ii) denotes the volume number, and the Arabic numeral (95) the page number. Thus the reference D.ii.95 is to volume two, page 95, of the Dīgha Nikāya. A small number of references with the prefix 'Vin' will also be encountered. These refer to a division of the Pali canon known as the Vinaya, which contains material relating to monastic law. Independent texts from the fifth collection of the Pali Canon (the Khuddaka Nikāya) such as the *Sutta Nipāta*, also have their own abbreviations (in this case Sn). A capital letter A after any of the above abbreviations (such as DA or VA in the case of the Vinaya) means the reference is to the commentary (*aṭṭhakathā*) on the text in question.

Translations of the Pali canon into English have been published by the Pali Text Society, and more recent translations are available from Wisdom Publications. Translations of other texts cited are mentioned in the References section for each chapter, and a Google search will usually reveal a wide selection of online translations for most of the sources mentioned.

Language and pronunciation

Buddhist texts were composed in and translated into many languages, including Pali, Sanskrit, Tibetan, Thai, Burmese, Chinese, Japanese, and Korean. The convention followed here is to cite Buddhist technical terms in their Sanskrit forms except when the discussion refers to Pali sources when Pali forms are used. Transliteration from languages such as Sanskrit and Pali requires the use of diacritics. This is because the twenty-six letters of the English alphabet are insufficient to represent the larger number of characters in Indic languages. A horizontal line (macron) above a vowel lengthens it, such that the character 'a' is pronounced as in 'far' rather than 'fat'. For the most part, the other marks do not affect pronunciation sufficiently to be of any concern, with the following exceptions:

c pronounced 'ch' as in 'choose'
ś or ṣ pronounced 'sh' as in 'shoes'
ñ pronounced 'ny' as in Spanish 'mañana'

A dot beneath a consonant (ṭ, ḍ, etc.) indicates that the tongue touches the roof of the mouth when pronouncing these letters, to give the characteristic sound of English when spoken with an Indian accent.

Translations without attribution are my own.

Chapter 1
Buddhist morality

Morality is woven into the fabric of Buddhist teachings and there is no major branch or school of Buddhism that fails to emphasize the importance of the moral life. The scriptures of Buddhism in many languages speak eloquently of virtues such as non-violence and compassion, and the Buddhist 'Golden Rule' (e.g. *Dhammapada* 130) counsels us not to do anything to others we would not like done to ourselves. Newcomers to Buddhism are often struck by the variety of the different Asian traditions, as divergent in form as Zen and Tibetan Buddhism, but underlying these differences we can discern a common moral core composed of the principles, precepts, virtues, and values expounded by the Buddha in the 5th century BCE. The purpose of this first chapter is to review these moral teachings which today guide the conduct of some 500 million Buddhists around the world (Figure 1).

Dharma and karma

The ultimate foundation for Buddhist ethics is Dharma. Dharma is a term with many meanings, but its most basic sense is that of a principle of cosmic order. Every aspect of life is believed to be regulated by Dharma, from the succession of the seasons to the norms that govern human societies. Dharma is neither caused by nor under the control of a supreme being, and the gods themselves are subject to its ordinances, as was the Buddha (the Buddha

1

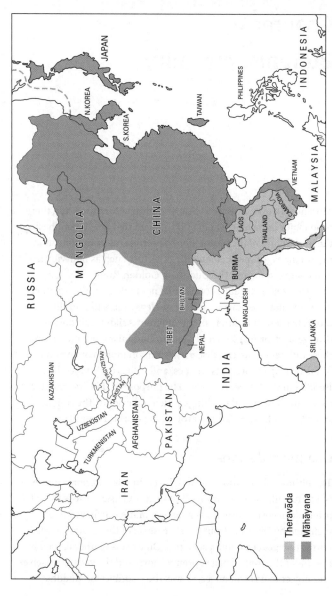

1. Map of Buddhism in Asia.

claimed only to have discovered Dharma, not to have invented it).
Living in accordance with Dharma and implementing its
requirements with respect to law, custom, religion, and ethics is
thought to lead to happiness and well-being; neglecting or
transgressing it is said to lead to endless suffering in the cycle of
rebirth known as *saṃsāra*.

'Dharma' is also the name given to Buddhist teachings, since these
are believed to reflect the truth about the nature of things. In his
first sermon, the Buddha was said to have 'turned the wheel of
Dharma' and in this discourse he set out the Four Noble Truths
(see Box 1), the last of which is the Noble Eightfold Path that leads
to nirvana. This path has three divisions—Morality (*śīla*),
Meditation (*samādhi*), and Wisdom (*prajñā*)—from which we can
see that morality is a foundational component of the path to
nirvana. The traditional enumeration of the eight items that make
up the path begins with Wisdom, as shown in Box 2, since one
cannot meaningfully embark on the path without at least a
preliminary understanding of Buddhist teachings.

Dharma embodies a moral order commonly referred to as the 'law
of karma' (*karma-niyāma*). In popular usage karma is thought of
simply as the good and bad things that happen to a person, a bit
like good and bad luck. However, this oversimplifies what for
Buddhists is a complex concept embracing both ethics and
cosmology. The literal meaning of the Sanskrit word karma is

Box 1 The Four Noble Truths

Duḥkha—All existence is suffering.
Samudaya—Suffering is caused by craving.
Nirodha—Suffering can have an end.
Marga—The way to the end of suffering is the Noble Eightfold
Path.

'action', but when used in an ethico-religious context karma is concerned exclusively with moral actions and the way they affect individuals in present and future lives. Karma is not a system of rewards and punishments meted out by God but an impersonal moral law. It is thought to be objective, in the way that scientific laws are objective, but unlike the laws of science the law of karma is not value-free: it embodies a principle of justice which ensures that good actions have good consequences and bad actions bad ones. In this way everyone in the end receives their just deserts.

The consequences of karma take two forms, which we might call transitive and intransitive. The transitive effect is seen in the impact moral actions have on others; for example, when we kill or steal, someone is deprived of her life or property. The intransitive effect is seen in the way moral actions affect the agent. According to Buddhism, human beings have free will, and in the exercise of free choice they engage in self-determination. By freely and repeatedly choosing in certain ways individuals shape their characters, and through their characters their futures. As the proverb has it: 'Sow an act, reap a habit; sow a habit, reap a character; sow a character, reap a destiny.'

Box 2 The Eightfold Path and its Three Divisions

1. **Right View**	**Wisdom (*prajñā*)**
2. **Right Resolve**	
3. **Right Speech**	**Morality (*śīla*)**
4. **Right Action**	
5. **Right Livelihood**	
6. **Right Effort**	**Meditation (*samādhi*)**
7. **Right Mindfulness**	
8. **Right Meditation**	

The consequences of karmic choices are referred to as the 'maturation' (*vipāka*) or 'fruit' (*phala*) of the karmic act. The metaphor is an agricultural one: performing moral actions is like planting seeds that will bear fruit at a later date. It is not hard to see how even within the course of a single lifetime habitual patterns of behaviour lead to predictable results. Great works of literature reveal how the fate that befalls the protagonists is often due not to chance but to a character flaw that leads to a tragic series of events. In the plays of Shakespeare, for example, Othello's jealousy, Macbeth's ruthless ambition, and Hamlet's hesitation and self-doubt would all be seen by Buddhists as karmic seeds, and the tragic outcome in each case the inevitable 'fruit' of the choices these character traits predisposed the protagonists to make. Individuals are thus to a large extent the authors of their own good and bad fortune.

Not all the consequences of what a person does are experienced in the lifetime in which the deeds are performed. Karma that has been accumulated but not yet experienced is carried forward to the next life, or even many lifetimes ahead. Accordingly, certain aspects of a person's next rebirth are thought of as karmically determined. These include the family into which one is born, one's social status, physical appearance, and of course, one's character and personality, since these are simply carried over from the previous life. The doctrine of karma, however, does not claim that everything that happens to a person is determined in advance. Many of the things that happen in life—like catching a cold—may simply be random events or accidents. Karma does not determine precisely what will happen or how anyone will react to what happens, which means that individuals are free to resist previous conditioning and establish new patterns of behaviour.

What, then, makes an action good or bad? The Buddha defined karma by reference to intentions and the acts consequent upon them. He stated, 'It is intention (*cetanā*), O monks, that I call karma; having willed one acts through body, speech, or mind'

(A iii.415). From this we see that intention is an important moral criterion. Also important are the three motivational factors that according to Buddhist psychology underlie and shape intention. These are known as 'roots' (*mūla*)—again we note the agricultural metaphor—and there are said to be three good roots and three bad roots. The bad (*akuśala*) roots are greed (*rāga*), hatred (*dveṣa*), and delusion (*moha*), and the good (*kuśala*) roots are their opposites, namely non-attachment, benevolence, and understanding.

The psychological factors just described constitute what we might call the 'subjective' criteria of right action. Acting morally, however, is not simply a question of meaning well or of having good intentions. There is also an objective criterion, namely that good intentions find expression in actions that are in accordance with Dharma. As Buddhism explains it, these are basically actions that do no harm to oneself or others and find approval among the wise. Actions that fulfil these two criteria produce good karma while actions that fail in this respect produce bad karma and are prohibited in various sets of precepts, about which more will be said below.

Buddhists speak of good karma as 'merit' (*puṇya*), and much effort is expended in acquiring it (its opposite, bad karma, is known as *pāpa*). Some Buddhists picture merit as a kind of spiritual capital—like money in a bank account—whereby credit is built up as the deposit on a heavenly rebirth. As we will see, one of the best ways for a layperson to earn merit is by supporting the *saṅgha*, or order of monks. Merit can even be made by congratulating other donors and rejoicing in their generosity. Some Buddhists make the accumulation of merit an end in itself and go to the extreme of carrying a notebook to keep a tally of their karmic 'balance'. This is to lose sight of the fact that merit is earned as a by-product of doing what is right. To do good deeds simply to obtain good karma would be to act from a selfish motive and would not earn much merit.

In many Buddhist cultures there is a belief in 'merit transference', or the idea that good karma can be shared with others, just like money. Donating good karma also has the happy result that instead of one's own karmic balance being depleted, as it would in the case of money, it increases as a result of the generous motivation in sharing. The more one gives, the more one receives! It is doubtful to what extent there is canonical authority for notions of this kind, although the motivation to share one's merit in a spirit of generosity is certainly karmically wholesome and would lead to the formation of a generous and benevolent character.

Precepts

In common with Indian tradition as a whole, Buddhism expresses its ethical requirements in the form of duties rather than rights. The most general moral duties are those found in the Five Precepts (Box 3), for example the duty to refrain from evil acts

Box 3 The Five Precepts (*pañcaśīla*)

This is the most widely known list of precepts in Buddhism, comparable in importance to the Ten Commandments of Christianity. The Five Precepts are undertaken as voluntary commitments in the ceremony of 'going for refuge' when a person becomes a Buddhist.

They are as follows:
1. I undertake the precept to refrain from harming living creatures.
2. I undertake the precept to refrain from taking what has not been given.
3. I undertake the precept to refrain from sexual misconduct.
4. I undertake the precept to refrain from speaking falsely.
5. I undertake the precept to refrain from taking intoxicants.

such as killing and stealing. These duties are thought of as implicit requirements of Dharma, and on becoming a Buddhist one formally 'takes' (or accepts) the precepts in a ritual known as 'going for refuge'.

Apart from the Five Precepts, various other lists of precepts are found, such as the Eight Precepts (*aṣṭāṅga-śīla*) and the Ten Precepts (*daśa-śīla*). These are commonly adopted as additional commitments on the twice-monthly holy days (*poṣadha*) and supplement the first four of the Five Precepts with additional restrictions, such as the time when meals may be taken. Another similar set of precepts is the Ten Good Paths of Action (*daśa-kuśala-karmapatha*). Precepts like these which apply to the laity are comparatively few compared to those observed by monks and nuns, as explained below.

Vinaya

A term often found paired with Dharma is Vinaya. Particularly in early sources, the compound 'Dharma-Vinaya' ('doctrine and discipline') is used to denote the whole body of Buddhist teachings and practice. Originally, the Buddhist monastic order (*saṅgha*) formed a small group within a broad community of wandering teachers and students known as *parivrājakas* ('wanderers') or *śramaṇas* ('strivers'). From these simple beginnings evolved a complex code for the regulation of monastic life comparable to the Rule of Saint Benedict observed by Benedictine monks in the West. In Buddhism, the rules became formulated in a portion of the canon known as the Vinaya Piṭaka. The Vinaya Piṭaka also contains a large number of stories and biographical material relating to the Buddha, as well as a certain amount of historical matter regarding the *saṅgha*.

The purpose of the Vinaya is to regulate life within the communities of monks and nuns and govern their relationship with the laity. In its final form the text is divided into three sections, the first of which contains the set of rules—over 200 in number—for monks and nuns. This is known as the *Prātimokṣa*, and consists of an inventory of offences organized into seven categories according to seriousness. It embraces not only moral questions, such as lying and stealing, but also matters of dress, etiquette, and general deportment. Many scholars now agree that the *Prātimokṣa* seems to have undergone at least three stages of development: as a simple confession of faith recited by Buddhist monks and nuns at periodic intervals; as a bare monastic code ensuring proper monastic discipline; and as a monastic liturgy, representing a period of relatively high organization and structure within the *saṅgha*. This inventory of offences became formalized into a communally chanted liturgy known as the *Prātimokṣa-sūtra*, which is recited as a kind of public declaration of virtue at the *poṣadha*, or fast-day ceremony on the new and the full moon days each month.

Virtues

Although the precepts, whether lay or monastic, are of great importance, there is more to the Buddhist moral life than following rules. Rules must not only be followed but followed for the right reasons and with the correct motivation. It is here that the role of the virtues becomes important, and Buddhist morality as a whole may be likened to the two sides of a coin: on one side are the precepts and on the other the virtues. The precepts, in fact, may be thought of simply as a list of things a virtuous person would never do. The task of the virtues is to counteract negative dispositions called *kleśas* or vices. The lengthy lists of virtues and vices that appear in Buddhist scholastic literature are extrapolated from the cluster of three 'root' or 'cardinal' virtues mentioned above, namely non-attachment (*arāga*), benevolence (*adveṣa*), and understanding (*amoha*). While these are the three most basic Buddhist virtues, there are many others, three of the most important of which are non-harming or non-injury (*ahiṃsā*), generosity (*dāna*), and compassion (*karuṇā*).

Early sources emphasize the importance of cultivating correct dispositions and habits so that moral conduct becomes the natural and spontaneous manifestation of internalized beliefs and values, rather than simple conformity to external rules. Many formulations of the precepts make this clear. Of someone who follows the first precept it is said, 'Laying aside the stick and the sword he dwells compassionate and kind to all living creatures' (D.i.4). Abstention from taking life or causing harm (*ahiṃsā*) therefore ideally flows from a compassionate identification with living things, rather than as a constraint imposed contrary to natural inclination. To observe the first precept perfectly requires a profound understanding of the relationship between living beings (according to Buddhism, in the long cycle of rebirth we have all been each other's fathers, mothers, sons, and so forth) coupled with an unswerving disposition of universal benevolence and compassion.

In India, the concept of non-harming (*ahiṃsā*) seems to have originated among the unorthodox renouncer movements, in other words among non-Brahmanical schools like Buddhism and Jainism. These placed greater emphasis on concern (*dayā*) and sympathy (*anukampā*) for living creatures inspired by empathy based on the awareness that others dislike pain and death just as much as oneself. Animal sacrifice, which had played an important part in religious rites in India from ancient times, was rejected by both Buddhism and Jainism as cruel and barbaric. Due in part to their influence, blood sacrifices in the orthodox Brahmanical tradition came increasingly to be replaced by symbolic offerings such as vegetables, fruit, and milk. Many Buddhists—especially followers of the Mahāyāna in East Asia—have embraced vegetarianism (discussed further in Chapter 3) since this diet does not involve the slaughter of animals.

Among the Indian renouncers, the practice of *ahiṃsā* was sometimes taken to extremes. Jain monks took the greatest precautions against destroying tiny forms of life such as insects, even unintentionally. Their practices had some influence on Buddhism; for example, Buddhist monks often used a strainer to make sure they did not destroy small creatures in their drinking-water. These are the small creatures the Buddha had in mind when he said he 'was full of pity even for a drop of water' (M.i.79). Monks also avoided travel during the monsoon so they would not tread on insects and other small creatures that become abundant after the rains.

Concern is even apparent in early sources about the practice of agriculture because of the inevitable destruction of life caused by ploughing the earth. In general, however, Buddhism regards the destruction of life as morally wrong only when it is caused intentionally (in other words, when the death of creatures is the outcome sought). Due to its association with *ahiṃsā*, Buddhism is generally perceived as non-violent and peace-loving, an impression that is to a large extent correct. While Buddhist countries have not been free from war and conflict, as we shall see in Chapter 5, Buddhist teachings constantly praise non-violence and express disapproval of killing or causing injury.

One of the most important virtues, for lay Buddhists in particular, is *dāna*. The term is related to the English word 'donor' and means 'giving', or 'generosity'. The primary recipient of lay Buddhist generosity is the *saṅgha*—since monks and nuns possess nothing, they are entirely dependent upon the laity for support. The laity provides all the material needs of the monastic community, everything from food, robes, and medicine to the land and buildings which constitute the monastic residence. In the *kaṭhina* ceremony, which takes place following the annual monsoon retreat in countries where Theravāda Buddhism is practised, cotton cloth is supplied to the monks by the laity for the purpose of making robes. Such donations are thought to generate merit (*puṇya*). The relationship is not just one-way, for in return monks perform religious ceremonies and provide Dharma teachings, and the gift of the Dharma is said to be the highest of all gifts.

At all levels of society—between family members, friends, and even strangers—generosity is widely encouraged and seen as an indication of spiritual development. This is because the generous person, as well as being free from egocentric thoughts and sensitive to the needs of others, finds it easier to practise renunciation and cultivate an attitude of detachment. The story of Prince Vessantara, hero of the popular *Vessantara Jātaka*, is well known in South Asia. Vessantara gave away everything he owned, even down to his wife and children! Many Theravāda sources praise *dāna,* and Mahāyāna sources emphasize the extreme generosity of bodhisattvas, who are disposed to give away even parts of their bodies, or their lives, in order to aid others. As we shall see, *dāna* is also the first of the 'Six Perfections' (*pāramitā*) of a bodhisattva.

Mahāyāna morality

The Mahāyāna was a major movement in the history of Buddhism that emerged around the start of the common era. While the Mahāyāna developed new teachings, it is not a monolithic system, and there is no one 'official' code of ethics for either laymen or monks. The Vinayas of the early schools were not rejected and continued to be observed by monks and nuns alongside the new teachings recommended for bodhisattvas in Mahāyāna *sūtras*.

The Mahāyāna subsumed the earlier ethical teachings under an expanded framework of its own, within which three levels were identified. The first level was known as 'Moral Discipline' (*saṃvara-śīla*) and consists of the observance of moral precepts of the kind already noted. The second level is known as the 'Cultivation of Virtue' (*kuśala-dharma-saṃgrāhaka-śīla*) and is concerned with the accumulation of the virtues and other good qualities necessary for the attainment of nirvana. The third category is 'Altruistic Conduct' (*sattva-artha-kriyā-śīla*) and consists of moral action directed to the needs of others.

The Mahāyāna claimed that the early followers had not advanced much beyond the first level and that their moral practices were deficient in lacking concern for the well-being of others. In the Mahāyāna, the bodhisattva who devotes himself to the service of others becomes the new paradigm for religious practice, as opposed to the *arhat*, or saint in the early tradition, who is now criticized (somewhat unfairly) for leading a cloistered life devoted to the self-interested pursuit of liberation. The Mahāyāna bodhisattva practises six virtues known as the 'Six Perfections' (*pāramitā*) listed in Box 4. Three of these (*śīla, samādhi*, and *prajñā*) coincide with the three divisions of the Eightfold Path of early Buddhism, demonstrating both continuity and innovation in the evolving moral tradition.

The virtue of compassion (*karuṇā*) is important in all schools of Buddhism but is particularly emphasized by the Mahāyāna. In early Buddhism, *karuṇā* figures as the second of the four *Brahma-vihāras,* or 'sublime attitudes'. These are states of mind cultivated through the practice of meditation. The four are loving-kindness (*maitrī*), compassion (*karuṇā*), sympathetic joy (*muditā*), and equanimity (*upekṣā*). The practice of the four *Brahma-vihāras* involves radiating outwards the positive qualities of each, directing them first towards oneself, then to one's family, the local community, and eventually to all beings in the universe.

Box 4 The Six Perfections (*pāramitā*)

1. **Generosity (*dāna*)**
2. **Morality (*śīla*)**
3. **Patience (*kṣānti*)**
4. **Perseverance (*vīrya*)**
5. **Meditation (*samādhi*)**
6. **Wisdom (*prajñā*)**

In Mahāyāna iconography and art, the symbolic embodiment of compassion is the great bodhisattva Avalokiteśvara, 'the one who looks down from on high' (see Figure 2). He is portrayed as having a thousand arms extending in all directions to minister to those in need and is appealed to for help by those in difficult circumstances. In the course of time there appeared a doctrine of salvation by faith according to which the mere invocation of the name of a Buddha was sufficient, given the extent of the Buddha's compassion, to ensure rebirth in a 'Pure Land', or heaven.

An important innovation in Mahāyāna ethics was the doctrine of 'skilful means' (*upāya-kauśalya*). The roots of this notion are found in the Buddha's skill in teaching the Dharma, demonstrated in his ability to adapt his message to the context in which it was delivered. For example, when talking to Brahmins, the Buddha

2. The Bodhisattva Avalokiteśvara, the embodiment of compassion.

would often explain his teachings by reference to their rituals and traditions, leading his audience step by step to see the truth of a Buddhist tenet. Parables, metaphors, and similes formed an important part of his teaching repertoire, skilfully tailored to the level of his audience. The Mahāyāna developed this idea in a radical way by intimating, in texts such as the *Lotus Sūtra* (*circa* 1st century CE), that the early teachings were not just skilfully delivered, but were a means to an end in their entirety in the sense that they contained nothing that could not be modified to suit the demands of changing situations.

This idea has certain implications for ethics. If the teachings the Buddha had given were provisional rather than ultimate, then perhaps the precepts they contain could also be of a provisional nature. Thus, the clear and strict rules encountered in the early sources could be interpreted more in the way of guidelines rather than as ultimately binding. In particular, bodhisattvas—the new moral heroes of the Mahāyāna—could claim increased latitude based on the importance of compassion. A bodhisattva takes a vow to save all beings, and there is evidence in many texts of impatience with rules which seem to get in the way of a bodhisattva going about his salvific mission. The new imperative was to act in accordance with the spirit rather than the letter of the precepts, and some sources go so far as to allow compassion (*karuṇā*) to override the precepts and sanction immoral acts if the bodhisattva sees that so doing would prevent or reduce suffering.

According to one early source, the Skill-in-Means Sūtra (*Upāya-kauśalya-sūtra*) dating to around the 1st century BCE, even killing is justified to prevent someone committing a heinous crime and suffering karmic retribution in hell. Elsewhere, telling lies, abandoning celibacy, and other breaches of the precepts are said to be permissible in exceptional circumstances. It is not always clear whether such behaviour is held up by the texts as a model for imitation, or simply as a vivid illustration of the great compassion of bodhisattvas who willingly accept the karmic consequences of breaking the precepts as the price of helping others.

In Tantric teachings, too, moral precepts are sometimes set aside. Tantra, also known as the Vajrayāna ('Diamond Vehicle') or Mantrayāna ('Vehicle of Mantras'), is a form of Buddhism that developed in India in the 6th century CE and is characterized by antinomianism (the reversal of moral norms) and the use of magical techniques that aim to speed the practitioner to enlightenment in a single lifetime. Tantra aims to transmute negative mental energies into positive ones using a form of mystical alchemy that is believed to transform the whole personality. By liberating energy trapped at an instinctual level in emotions such as fear and lust, it was thought that practitioners could do the psychological equivalent of splitting the atom and use the energy produced to propel themselves rapidly to enlightenment.

In certain forms of Tantra, such practices involved the deliberate and controlled reversal of moral norms and the breaking of taboos in order to help jolt the mind out of its conventional patterns of thought into a higher state of awareness. Examples of such activities include drinking alcohol and sexual intercourse, both serious breaches of the monastic rules. While some practitioners understood such teachings and practices literally, however, others saw them as merely symbolic and useful subjects for meditation.

From the above we can see that while some aspects of Buddhist morality are far from unique (prohibitions on killing, stealing, and lying are found in moral codes the world over), others—like belief in karma and rebirth—are less familiar, at least in the West. In Chapter 2 we consider how students of Western ethics have sought to understand and classify this complex body of moral teachings.

Chapter 2
Ethics East and West

It is only since Buddhism arrived in the West that a nascent discipline of Buddhist ethics has developed. Its emergence can conveniently be dated to 1964 and the publication of a book by Winston King titled *In the Hope of Nibbāna: The Ethics of Theravāda Buddhism*. Since then, scholars have had recourse to various Western theories in the hope of gaining a deeper insight into the nature of Buddhist ethics. Such attempts are not without their problems, for instance there may be cultural, historical, and conceptual differences that distort or invalidate any attempt to compare Western and Eastern ethics. We will encounter an example of this towards the end of the chapter when we discuss the concept of rights. First, however, we review the main branches of Western ethics and their aims.

Ethics may be said to have three main branches: (i) descriptive ethics; (ii) normative ethics; and (iii) metaethics. Broadly speaking, the job of the first is to give an objective account of the moral prescriptions, norms, and values of a community or group and to show how action-guiding precepts and principles are applied in specific contexts. The second branch, normative ethics, proposes general rules and principles governing how we *ought* to act and tries to define the character and shape of the 'good life'. It also offers justification and validation for the norms it seeks to establish. Finally, metaethics sees its task as providing conceptual clarification by analysing the meaning of moral terms, and considering the overall coherence of the various elements of an ethical system such as its moral psychology, theory of action, and values.

Applying this classification to the present volume, in setting out the moral teachings of Buddhism, Chapter 1 was concerned mainly with descriptive ethics; the present chapter discusses questions broadly of a metaethical nature; and the remainder of the volume addresses problems in normative ethics. Since our focus will be primarily on the application of normative principles to particular issues (e.g. abortion, euthanasia, ecology, and war), we could say that the main focus of this book is *applied normative ethics*.

Three ethical theories

Three of the most influential theories of ethics in the West have been deontology, utilitarianism, and virtue ethics. Immanuel Kant (1724–1804) is the most famous exponent of deontological ethics, an approach that emphasizes notions of duty and obligation and is characterized by looking backwards for justification. For example, a deontologist might suggest that the reason I am morally obliged to give some money to Tom is because I promised to do so when I borrowed it from him yesterday. My promise in the past thus gave rise to a moral obligation which I now have a duty to discharge. Deontological systems of ethics typically emphasize rules, commandments, and precepts which impose obligations we have a duty to fulfil.

By contrast, utilitarianism—a theory closely associated with Jeremy Bentham (1748–1832) and John Stuart Mill (1806–73)—seeks justification in the future through the good consequences expected to flow from the performance of an act. Utilitarians would justify the repayment of my debt by pointing to the satisfaction it will give Tom to have his money returned, the benefit of the maintenance of our friendship, the advantage of being able to ask Tom for another loan if the need arises, and the general good to society as a whole that flows from people keeping promises and paying debts. They will weigh up these consequences against the disadvantages of not repaying the loan—such as the loss of friendship, confidence, and trust—and conclude that the former is preferable and hence the morally correct choice.

According to virtue ethics, of which Aristotle (384–322 BCE) was a leading exponent, what is of primary importance in ethics is neither pre-existing obligations nor pleasant outcomes, but the development of character so that a person becomes habitually and spontaneously good. Virtue ethics seeks a transformation of the personality through the development of correct habits: the way to act rightly, according to virtue ethics, is not simply to follow certain kinds of rules, nor seek pleasant consequences, but first and foremost to *be* or *become* a certain kind of person. As this transformation proceeds, the virtuous person may well find that her behaviour spontaneously comes into line with moral norms of the kind familiar in deontological systems of ethics. She may also find that an increase in happiness is another consequence of her conduct, since not infrequently it turns out that a person who adopts a consistent plan of life and lives according to a consciously chosen and integrated set of values will be the happier for it. Aristotle called the state of well-being that results from living rightly *eudaimonia*, a term often translated as 'happiness' but which really means something like 'thriving' or 'flourishing'. Perhaps we can see a similarity (at least a conceptual one) between this state and the Buddhist goal of nirvana.

The above much-simplified account does not do justice to the breadth and sophistication of the three theories considered. Its purpose, however, is merely to show that they each capture some aspect of Buddhist morality as outlined in Chapter 1. Thus, Buddhism possesses features associated with deontological ethics, as can be seen from the emphasis on the Five Precepts as moral rules that should never be infringed. The no-harm principle (*ahiṃsā*) imposes a duty to avoid causing injury, and the understanding of karma as a universal moral law suggests an interpretation of Buddhist ethics along Kantian lines.

At the same time, belief in karma also gives Buddhism something of a utilitarian flavour since it suggests that the point of moral action is to create happiness and well-being in present and future lives. Or, to put it slightly differently, we could say that the aim is to secure our release from suffering (*duḥkha*), the objective mentioned in the Third Noble Truth. On this understanding, since the performance of good deeds leads to the avoidance of painful consequences, Buddhism could be classified as a form of 'negative utilitarianism'.

We also find similarities with virtue ethics. Buddhism can be seen as teaching a path of self-transformation (the Eightfold Path) that seeks the elimination of negative states (or vices) like greed, hatred, and delusion, and their replacement by positive or wholesome ones (virtues). The transformation of the ordinary person (*pṛthagjana*) into a Buddha is believed to come about progressively over many lifetimes through the cultivation of the virtues we discussed in Chapter 1, leading step by step to the goal of complete self-realization known as nirvana.

Each of the three theories considered provides a partial fit, but none provides a fully comprehensive explanation. Perhaps, then, Buddhist morality is not exclusively a matter of obligations, consequences, or virtues, but to some extent all three.

Particularism

Recognizing that morality is complex in the way just stated, some scholars feel that a more flexible approach is needed if we are to understand Buddhist ethics correctly. On this basis Charles

Hallisey has suggested that Buddhists did not follow any *one* ethical theory but 'adopted a kind of ethical particularism'. Ethical particularism is a pluralistic theory of ethics developed by Scottish philosopher W. D. Ross (1877–1971). It postulates certain general or 'prima facie' duties that are then applied intuitively as the context demands. These duties are summed up by Ross in the form of seven guiding principles like non-injury (we should refrain from harming others), beneficence (we should always be kind to others), self-improvement (we should strive to improve our own well-being), and justice (we should always try to be fair).

Clearly, in terms of values there is not much here that Buddhism would disagree with, and a Particularist interpretation has the added advantage of validating the Mahāyāna doctrine of skilful means by allowing that beneficence (or compassion) can sometimes take priority over non-injury. Thus, Particularism would suggest that while recognizing the importance of general duties (like deontology), good outcomes (like utilitarianism), and self-development (like virtue ethics), Buddhists prize a nuanced sense of judgement (or 'practical wisdom') that allows them to act appropriately as circumstances demand. While Particularism has the merit of highlighting the importance of context, however, it seems to pay insufficient attention to the *a priori* nature of Dharma. Buddhism—unlike Existentialism—does not believe that moral choices are validated solely through the act of choosing. Even if our intuition tells us we are acting for the best, our moral compass may be misaligned, and certain choices may create bad karma because despite our best intentions they are contrary to Dharma. The situations Particularists seek to negotiate on a case-by-case basis may therefore not be entirely morally unconstrained in the way they imagine.

Perfectionism

Another way of classifying Buddhist ethics is by reference to an ethical theory known as Perfectionism. The aim of Perfectionism is, as we might say today, 'to be the best version of oneself one can'. Virtue ethics is a form of Perfectionism since it identifies the good with the perfection of qualities like generosity and wisdom. In developing such qualities, we emulate the conduct of role models like revered teachers, saints, or Buddhas. This form of Perfectionism is characterized as 'agent-centred' since it envisages individuals as prioritizing their own perfection.

Some Perfectionists, however, focus less on the individual and believe that what should be perfected are overall states of affairs such as general happiness or well-being. The goal of this 'agent-neutral' Perfectionism is making the world a better place. This might be achieved through developments in art and science, economics, politics, or in other ways that benefit the community as a whole.

It is possible to interpret Buddhism as a form of Perfectionism in either of the above ways. Early Buddhism corresponds more closely to agent-centred Perfectionism since the goal is generally depicted as that of personal salvation through virtuous self-transformation. Mahāyāna Buddhism, on the other hand, bears a greater resemblance to agent-neutral Perfectionism since the moral imperative is to increase universal happiness by eliminating suffering for all beings. Of course, the selfless bodhisattvas who dedicate themselves to this ideal also need to develop virtues like wisdom and compassion, so perhaps Buddhist ethics could be characterized as an agent-neutral form of 'character consequentialism'.

While all the theories we have considered have their merits, they also have limitations. This has led some scholars to claim Buddhist ethics is *sui generis* and transcends any and all classification in terms of Western theories. The search for an overarching Western template, they believe, is doomed to failure. But perhaps this is unduly pessimistic. In particular, if we compare Buddhism with other systems of *religious* ethics (in contrast to the various secular theories mentioned so far) the theoretical differences do not seem so great.

Thus, like Buddhism, Christian ethics has a well-defined deontological component (as seen in the ten commandments), and (like utilitarianism) also values pleasant consequences (notably eternal happiness in heaven). The virtues also form a central part of Christian ethical teachings (e.g. the virtues of faith, hope, and charity). Other religions (e.g. Hinduism and Islam) also combine these ethical components in various ways but are not on this account thought to be *sui generis*. While individual religions vary in their moral teachings, the fact that they can be seen as pluralist at a theoretical level suggests that Buddhist ethics is not totally unique or capable of being understood exclusively 'in its own terms'. The challenge, then, at least as more optimistic interpreters see it, is to determine which meta-theory, or permutation of the theories we have considered, provides the best explanation.

The absence of 'ethics'

It would be helpful if we could ask Buddhists themselves for guidance on where their religion stands on questions of the above kind. However, there is a curious absence of authoritative opinion on these matters. The great thinkers of the past left no legacy in the form of treatises on ethics, and there is not even a word for 'ethics' in the early Indian texts—the closest approximation is *śīla*, often translated as 'morality' but closer in meaning to disciplined behaviour or self-restraint. While Buddhist thinkers developed sophisticated theories of metaphysics, epistemology, and logic, there never arose a branch of learning concerned with metaethics, or the philosophical analysis of moral norms. But what of the sources cited in Chapter 1 which speak of virtues and precepts—do these not have something to do with ethics? Indeed they do, but in the sense that as moral *teachings* they constitute the descriptive subject matter that is the starting point for normative reflection and metaethical analysis.

One of the few early texts to explore moral dilemmas is *Milinda's Questions*. This text dates to the beginning of the common era, and records a debate that took place in a Greek-influenced part of north-west India between a Buddhist monk (Nāgasena) and a Greek king (Milinda). In this text, in which the king plays the role of devil's advocate posing thorny questions to the monk, we see the beginnings of a line of ethical enquiry similar to the Socratic paradoxes in Plato's early dialogues. As an example of these, in the *Euthyphro*, Socrates asks whether certain things are good because they are loved by the gods, or whether they are loved by the gods because they are good. A Buddhist version of this dilemma might ask whether certain acts are good because they are rewarded by karma, or whether they are rewarded by karma because they are good. Unfortunately this was not one of the paradoxes posed by King Milinda in his discussion with Nāgasena, and the question was never framed in these terms by Buddhist thinkers.

Why ethics does not feature as a branch of philosophy in the canon of Buddhist learning is unclear. One suggestion is that since Buddhism began as a renouncer movement existing on the margins of society it was natural for it to remain disengaged from social and political affairs. In such a context there is not much need for ethical analysis. It may also be, as philosopher Christopher Gowans suggests, that Buddhists simply felt that moral theory was 'neither necessary nor even important to living morally and attaining enlightenment, and so they saw no reason to develop such a moral theory'. There are other possible reasons, and it is too soon to draw definitive conclusions on this point. Scholars, meanwhile, continue to explore intriguing parallels between Buddhism and other Western philosophical schools, as in the case of Stoicism (see Box 5).

Box 5 Stoicism

Stoicism is an ancient philosophy that is currently undergoing a revival. Stoicism was founded by the Greek philosopher Zeno (334–262 BCE) around a century after the death of the Buddha, and despite some differences (Stoics do not believe in karma and rebirth, or in a transcendent state like nirvana) there are similarities between the two. Both teach that life inevitably involves suffering, and that happiness can only be found by cultivating the right mental attitude in the face of adversity. For Stoics this means developing the four cardinal virtues of prudence (or practical wisdom), justice, temperance (or self-control), and fortitude. In this way one becomes indifferent to pleasure and pain and free from desire, which Stoics (like Buddhists) regard as the primary cause of suffering. As the Roman Stoic Seneca wrote in his *Letters from a Stoic*: 'Virtue is therefore the only good; she marches proudly between the two extremes of fortune, with great scorn for both.'

Stoics prioritize reason over dogma and seek to cultivate emotional resilience in the face of misfortune. They practise indifference or equanimity with respect to 'externals' such as wealth, reputation, health, and the other things in life that are beyond our control. As Marcus Aurelius (a Roman emperor of the 2nd century CE and author of the *Meditations*) expressed it, 'Almost nothing material is needed for a happy life, for he who understands existence.' Seeking to possess worldly goods or control external events, in the Stoic view, only leads to frustration and dissatisfaction. Replacing control with acceptance, according to the Stoics, is the way to achieve the state of happiness known as eudaimonia. Stoic techniques of mental discipline resemble Buddhist ones to some degree, and both have provided inspiration for contemporary training programmes in mindfulness and cognitive therapy.

Engaged Buddhism

More or less coinciding with the birth of Buddhist ethics was the appearance of a related movement known as 'engaged Buddhism'. While Buddhist ethics is concerned with the specifics of individual conduct, engaged Buddhism focuses on larger questions of public policy such as social justice, poverty, politics, and the environment. Clearly, there is a connection between them, and it can be no coincidence that both disciplines have arisen at roughly the same time as Buddhism encounters the West. Perhaps we can see Buddhist ethics and engaged Buddhism as corresponding to two major branches of Western thought—ethics and politics—which for one reason or another never attained an autonomous status in the canon of Buddhist learning.

Engaged Buddhism has become so important in modern Buddhism worldwide that one Buddhist scholar has argued that it has become a new 'vehicle', joining the previously identified three vehicles of Buddhism (Hīnayāna, Mahāyāna, and Vajrayāna). This does not mean to say that Buddhism has never been socially active, but rather that it is often perceived as passive in its approach to social problems. The promotion of engaged Buddhism owes much to the Vietnamese monk Thich Nhat Hanh, who coined the phrase 'socially engaged Buddhism' as a label for three Vietnamese ideas emphasizing awareness in daily life; social service; and social activism. This threefold emphasis not only establishes a connection with social, political, economic, and environmental issues, but also gives a sense of involving the ordinary lives of families and social communities. In this way, engaged Buddhism has an impact on the lives of individual Buddhists living 'in the world'. In calling for social justice many engaged Buddhists resort to the language of rights to express Buddhist demands. As discussed below, however, others doubt whether this quintessentially

Western discourse is the right medium in which to express Buddhist teachings.

Rights

At the beginning of the chapter we cautioned that cultural, historical, and conceptual differences might distort comparisons between Buddhist and Western ethics. The reader may also recall that in Chapter 1 we mentioned that Buddhism expresses its ethical requirements in the form of duties rather than rights. In the West, however, the vocabulary of rights has become the *lingua franca* of political and ethical discourse, and substantive moral claims are made and defended by appeal to rights. Thus, the abortion debate is commonly framed as a clash between 'the right to choose' and 'the right to life'. Proponents of euthanasia speak of the 'right to die', and minority rights are claimed in a plethora of contexts, such as 'gay' and 'transgender' rights. Some commentators, however, suggest that framing issues in these terms is inappropriate in the case of Buddhism.

A common objection is that the individualism implicit in rights is detrimental to both spiritual progress and social stability because it strengthens the ego and encourages selfish attitudes. Thus the renowned Thai Buddhist teacher P. A. Payutto has observed that Western notions of rights involve 'competition, mistrust and fear'. He and others worry that laying claim to individual rights conflicts with the Buddhist doctrine of 'no-self' (*anātman*): if there is ultimately no self, the argument goes, then who or what is the bearer of the rights in question? This is a complex issue, but a defender of rights might point out that the doctrine of no-self (*anātman*) only denies the existence of a transcendental self (*ātman*), not of a phenomenal, empirical self. It does not deny the existence of human individuals with unique self-shaped identities, and if such identities provide a foundation stable enough for the attribution of duties, as the Buddha clearly believed, presumably they also do for rights.

Doctrinal concerns about no-self, it might be added, do not hinder the demands of Buddhists who lay claim to rights, for example Buddhist refugees who claim a right to asylum or otherwise seek the protection of human rights instruments and charters. As far as the charge of individualism is concerned, moreover, it might be pointed out that human rights protect communities as much as individuals, and when Buddhist leaders like the Dalai Lama call for freedom of religion, they often do so on behalf of a nation like the people of Tibet.

Concern is often also expressed about the alien cultural provenance of the concept of rights, and particularly of human rights. In the 1990s, the political leaders of a number of Asian states (notably Malaysia, Indonesia, and Singapore, with strong backing from China) began to criticize the idea of human rights on grounds of its Western intellectual genealogy, seeing talk of such rights as merely a cover for imperialism and neo-colonialism. In place of rights they championed the idea of 'Asian values' which were said to be more community-oriented. Since then, Indian economist Amartya Sen has challenged the view that there is anything specifically 'Asian' about 'Asian values', and the Dalai Lama has repudiated the view that human rights 'cannot be applied to Asia and other parts of the Third World because of differences in culture and differences in social and economic development'. These authorities highlight commonalities in global ethical standards rather than differences.

These are simply examples of the arguments deployed on both sides. As the discussion shows, however, we should not simply assume that Western ethical concepts can be imported unproblematically into Buddhism. Some scholars even claim that Western epistemological categories like 'ethics' are themselves an obstacle to understanding Buddhist morality. Others are less pessimistic and hope that despite the pitfalls some mutual understanding will emerge. They find encouragement in the hermeneutics of German philosopher Hans-Georg Gadamer who asks, 'Is it not, in fact, the case that every misunderstanding presupposes a "deep common accord"?'

There are two main reasons why optimists believe metaethical enquiry into Buddhist ethics can be fruitful. The first is simple intellectual curiosity and a desire to understand whether the moral teachings we considered in Chapter 1 have a theoretical unity, and if so, what form it might take. While the jury is still out on this point, it seems at least worth asking the question. The second reason is practical, and is the same reason designers, engineers, and climate scientists produce models, prototypes, and simulations. They do this to test their designs and theories and make predictions about outcomes under a range of different scenarios.

The advantage of modelling Buddhist ethics is similar. In Chapter 8 we will consider issues like cloning, gene editing, and Transhumanism, subjects that for obvious reasons were never discussed in early Buddhist texts. If we can develop a working model of Buddhist ethics it at least gives us a starting point from which to address these issues. This is not to say that answers can be cranked out mechanically, and we must bear in mind the oft-quoted saying of statistician George E. P. Box (1919–2013) that 'all models are wrong, but some are useful'. Perhaps by overlaying the most useful parts of the theories discussed in this chapter we can arrive at a more robust model. No doubt it will need fine-tuning in the light of results, but it is better than approaching the challenges empty-handed.

Even if we manage to resolve the conceptual difficulties described in this chapter, however, we cannot assume, given the absence of any central ecclesiastical authority, that there will be unanimity among Buddhists on any given issue. Buddhists believe different things, come to different ethical conclusions based on their beliefs, and justify their conclusions in different ways. Determining what counts as the 'Buddhist view' on a topic is therefore problematic. We can, however, at least offer a few rules of thumb. Thus it seems reasonable to favour views which have strong support in authoritative textual sources; that represent the consensus among the majority of major schools; that have a broad cultural base; and have been consistently held over time. This still leaves much room for interpretation and disagreement, but it at least provides a starting point for discussion of the substantive issues that follow.

Chapter 3
Animals and the environment

Buddhism is often seen as an 'eco-friendly' religion with an expanded moral horizon encompassing not just human beings but also animals and the environment. As such, it is generally thought to have a more 'enlightened' attitude to nature than Christianity, which has traditionally taught that mankind is the divinely appointed steward of creation holding authority over the natural order. Writers such as historian Lynn White see this belief as one of the underlying causes of the contemporary ecological crisis, since it encourages the idea that nature exists simply to serve human interests and is there to be exploited as circumstances demand.

Buddhism, by contrast, is perceived as pursuing a path of harmonious integration with nature and as fostering identification and mutual respect within the natural world. Since, according to Buddhist teachings, human beings can be reborn as animals, and vice versa, the Buddhist world view suggests a much closer kinship between species. Because of this, Buddhism seems able to avoid the charge of 'speciesism', or of unfairly giving one species (human beings) priority over others.

A visitor to any Buddhist country will see many examples of spontaneous kindness towards animals. A custom common in many Buddhist countries is that of 'releasing life' (Chinese *fang sheng*), a practice whereby animals kept in captivity are released upon payment of a small fee. Typically, small birds are set free from their cages, and it is believed that merit is gained by the donor for this act of kindness. On a more theoretical level, the doctrine of dependent origination is interpreted by some as teaching that the entire cosmos has an underlying metaphysical unity that links all phenomena in a delicate and complex web of relationships. The image of 'Indra's net' found in the *Avataṃsaka Sūtra* (3rd–4th century CE) is often used to illustrate this concept, the net being a web of jewels which glisten and reflect one another in their many different facets creating a 'fractal' vision of reality.

While there may be some truth in the view that Buddhism is more benign in its attitude towards nature than Christianity, the idea that Buddhism is deeply in tune with 'green' values and a natural ally of the 'animal rights' and other activist movements requires qualification. There is no doubt that Buddhist literature contains many references to animals and the environment, but when the context of these references is examined, they often turn out to have little in common with the modern conservationist agenda or concern to reduce animal suffering. The liberation of human beings from suffering remains the primary focus of Buddhist teachings and in adopting what is in many respects an anthropocentric position (the view that value belongs to humans alone and nature is to be protected for their sake), the Buddhist view of nature may not be as far removed from the Christian one as is sometimes supposed.

The moral status of animals

At first sight, Buddhist texts appear to support the view that all living creatures must be respected. The first precept has a direct bearing on the treatment of animals since it prescribes non-violence not just towards human beings but to *prāṇa*, or 'living creatures'. The *Sutta Nipāta* categorically states:

> Having put down the rod toward all beings, toward those in the world
> both firm and frail, one should not kill living beings or cause to kill,
> nor should one approve of others who kill. (v. 394, trans. Bodhi)

The Buddha himself is portrayed as refraining from destroying
life and even from causing injury to seeds and plants (D.i.4). It is
often stated that enlightened beings 'show kindness and live
with compassion for the welfare of all living beings' (A.i.211).
Abstaining from violence is a requirement of the Eightfold Path
under the headings of Right Action and Right Livelihood.
Right Action is said to include abandoning the taking of life
(D. ii.312) and Right Livelihood forbids certain professions such
as trade in flesh and weapons (A.iii.208). A categorical ban is
imposed on hunting, butchering, and similar professions
(M.i.343). All the above directives clearly contribute to the
protection of animals.

Also influential in defining ethical attitudes towards the natural
world are the four *Brahma-vihāras*, mentioned in Chapter 1.
Referred to as the 'sublime attitudes', universal love (*maitrī*),
compassion (*karuṇā*), sympathetic joy (*muditā*), and equanimity
(*upekṣā*) foster feelings that lead to the protection of the natural
world and ensure its well-being. A truly compassionate person
would find it hard to reconcile these sentiments with callous
environmental damage and cruel blood sports. Though it
becomes clear in the reading of Buddhist texts that the sublime
attitudes are primarily prescribed for the spiritual advancement
of the practitioner (S.ii.264) rather than for the benefit of the
environment, it is also said that their practice gradually pervades
the whole world. Although the natural world is not the direct
object of these practices, then, it is at least an indirect beneficiary.
The Mahāyāna emphasis on the 'great compassion' (*mahā-karuṇā*)
of bodhisattvas, and the Yogācāra notion of the 'embryonic
Buddha' (*tathāgata-garbha*) which holds that the universal seed
of Buddhahood is present in all living beings, including animals,

further strengthen the ethical identification between oneself and the natural world that is vital to ecological concern.

The Buddhist values of non-violence and compassion are clearly expressed in the Buddha's opposition to animal sacrifice. Animal sacrifices are severely criticized and alternative sacrifices using oil, butter, and molasses are praised (D.i.141). The Buddha, on hearing that a great sacrifice was being planned that would include the slaughter of several animals, stated that no great merit would be gained from such an action (S.i.75). Yet although evincing concern for their suffering, Buddhist sources show little interest in understanding the nature of animals. It is clear they are held to suffer pain, but beyond that their status is ambiguous. Sometimes animal birth is praised (M.i.341), but most commonly it is denounced as brutish and lowly (M.iii.169). Not infrequently it is hinted that animals are moral beings that have the capacity to produce good and bad karma, and the Buddha once commented that a jackal he heard howling one morning had more gratitude and thankfulness than a particular monk he knew (S.ii.272).

Buddhist literary sources often misrepresent the true reality of animal life. In some texts, animals are given characteristics they do not have, and their biological reality is made obscure. This can be seen in an example from the *Jātakas*. The purpose of the *Jātaka* folktales is to impart moral lessons in the manner of Aesop's fables, but since animals and the natural world figure prominently in them, these tales are often quoted to demonstrate Buddhism's ecological credentials. The *Anta Jātaka*, for instance, is a tale showing the evil of flattery and greed. It describes the actions of a crow and a jackal, depicting them as greedy beings that resort to deceitful flattery in order to gain food (J.440–1). While the moral of the tale is salutary, the fact that animals are the main protagonists should not by itself be taken as evidence of Buddhist concern for animals. Quite the contrary, in fact, for in this case it universalizes the characteristics of greed and flattery as qualities shared by all members of the crow and jackal species. It categorically states in its accompanying verse that jackals are the lowest of all beasts and crows are the lowest of all birds. The anthropomorphic portrayal of these animals thus leads to a degradation of them that has little to do with ecological concern and may even undermine it.

This random association of moral qualities with certain species shows that Buddhism has little curiosity or interest in the animals themselves and uses them merely to represent *human* virtues and vices. In this respect, the more admirable characteristics of particular animals are sometimes applied to the Buddha and his followers. For example, the Buddha is compared to a bull-elephant who wanders alone (A.iv.435-7); his claim to enlightenment is likened to a lion's roar (A.ii.33); and his well-trained disciples are said to be like thoroughbred horses (A.i.244-6).

Plant life and wilderness

The ethical status of plant life in Buddhism is unclear. It is difficult to state definitively whether early Buddhists believed plants and vegetation to be on a par with other beings that suffer, or whether they were considered to be non-sentient. One detailed list of precepts includes a rule that forbids causing injury to seeds and plants (D.i.5), as mentioned earlier, and there are *Prātimokṣa* injunctions that prohibit damage to vegetation, classifying it as a form of life with a single sense-faculty (*eka-indriya jīva*) (Vin.iii.155). It is not clear, however, whether these rules have to do with ecology or public relations. Concern about lay expectations is evident in the Vinaya, and the laity would certainly have compared Buddhist monks with their Jain rivals (the Jains are famous even today for their strict discipline).

Elsewhere, bad karma is said to follow the cutting of a branch or tree that once gave fruit and shade (A.iii.369), and merit is promised to those who plant groves and parks (S.i.33). The great Buddhist emperor Aśoka (3rd century BCE) planted trees and medicinal herbs. Furthermore, in popular belief trees and plants merited respect as the abode of deities. This, however, remains an ambiguous criterion for ecology, for it could imply that a tree uninhabited by a deity can be cut down. It also suggests an interest in the protection of deities (theocentric) rather than the protection of trees (ecocentric).

As for the wilderness that forms an important part of the ecological agenda today, Buddhism gives no specific injunctions for its conservation, although references to wild nature are found. The Buddha described his Indian homeland in the following terms: 'delightful parks, groves, landscapes, and lotus ponds are few, while more numerous are the hills and slopes, rivers that are hard to cross, places with stumps and thorns, and rugged mountains' (A.i.35). For town- and village-dwellers the wilderness contained both real and imaginary dangers. Scholar Pia Brancaccio notes how 'The wilderness as a whole was regarded as a threat . . . The woods were populated by wild animals, ghosts, strange human beings, *yakṣas* [demons] and other living entities that nurtured the fears and fantasies of villagers. Buddhism, developing within growing urban communities, again perceived the sylvan environment with a mixture of fear and respect.' We also learn from the early sources that deforestation is not entirely a modern phenomenon: forests were exploited for timber (buildings were almost entirely made of wood), and by the Buddha's day large areas of the Ganges plain had been cleared for agricultural purposes.

The rugged nature of the wilderness, however, did not blind Buddhists to its beauty. The natural beauty of the Gosiṅga-sāla forest grove near Vesālī, full of perfumed trees in bloom, is described as very pleasing to the eye on a moonlit night (M.i.212). Since aesthetic arguments are often evoked in environmental ethics in order to justify preserving the wild beauty of nature, Buddhist aesthetics can be likewise employed. At the same time,

Buddhist literature also contains contrasting descriptions of opulent surroundings in which trees and ponds made of gold and other precious material are glorified (D.iii.182). Such descriptions suggest that the beauty of civilization was valued just as much as the beauty of the wilderness.

One of the most effective arguments for preserving the wilderness lies in what has come to be known as the 'hermit strand' in Buddhist literature. Identified by German scholar Lambert Schmithausen, this concerns the advice given to hermits to live in natural surroundings in order to pursue the path to liberation without distraction (e.g. M.i.274). The Buddha encouraged his monks to seek solitude in the jungle, saying, 'Here are the roots of trees, here are empty houses. Meditate monks! Do not be slothful and reproach yourselves later, this is my instruction to you' (A.iii.87). He himself left a palace to live in the forest, and the fact that the main events in his life—such as his birth, enlightenment, first sermon, and death—all took place under trees or in parks associates him with natural environments (Figure 3). The Buddha and his monks often took up residence in parks like the Jetavana near the town of Sāvatthi, a place described as 'not too near nor too far (from the town), with convenient access, quiet, remote from people, not crowded by day and quiet by night, suitable for spiritual practice' (Vin.i.39). Without such places, the religious seeker would be unable to seek refuge from active life, which seems to be one reason why the wilderness should be preserved. The basis of the hermit strand, however, is once again anthropocentric, and anthropocentrism is generally berated in environmental literature.

Equality or hierarchy?

One of the most important questions for an ethics concerned with the natural world has to do with which forms of life merit moral consideration. There is no clear Buddhist position on this issue,

3. **Buddha head in tree roots, Wat Mahathat, Ayutthaya, Thailand.**

but the view that all beings are equal in this respect is not easy to establish on Buddhist principles. It seems unlikely Buddhism would ally itself with the 'animal rights' movement since as we saw in Chapter 2 the concept of rights is an unfamiliar one. Even if it accepted the concept of rights, Buddhism is unlikely to regard the rights of animals and humans as equivalent because of its belief in a hierarchy among different forms of life. It is noteworthy that in monastic law, killing an animal is a minor (*pāyantika*) offence, while killing a human being is a much more serious one (a *pārājika*).

In the Buddhist description of *saṃsāra*, or the continuing cycle of rebirth, six realms, or *gatis*, are enumerated. These are hell, the animal realm, the ghostly world, the titans, human beings, and the heavenly realm (D.iii.264). Often represented in the 'wheel of life' (*bhavacakra*), three of these realms (those below the centre line) are classified as 'unfortunate' and three (those above the line) as 'fortunate' (see Figure 4).

4. The wheel of life.

Each of the six realms is accorded a separate status and nature. Animals occupy one realm and humans another, and it is clearly preferable to be born in the latter than the former. At the same time, there is a constant movement of beings within the different realms and no stage is permanent. It is worth noting, however, that a 'precious human rebirth' is given particular prestige, even greater than that of the gods. This is because whereas the gods are largely occupied in the passive enjoyment of karmic rewards, human beings have the ability, opportunity, and motivation to exercise free will and moral agency. For this reason, a human rebirth is the most auspicious of the six realms from which to attain liberation. However, even if humans have a unique value, it does not follow that *only* humans deserve moral respect: a hierarchical structure suggests a graduated scheme of value rather than a purely anthropocentric one.

With respect to the animal world, a point of some interest is how far down the chain of being our moral obligations extend. Early texts say that humans may be reborn as scorpions and centipedes

(A.v.289), or even worms and maggots (M.iii.168). The first precept, as mentioned earlier, prohibits causing injury to living creatures, but the boundaries of the moral world are fuzzy at the lower echelons. I have suggested elsewhere that the concept of 'karmic life' can provide a principle of demarcation. By 'karmic life' is meant those forms of life that are sentient, reincarnate, and are morally autonomous. This would include human beings and the higher mammals, but at the lower levels of the evolutionary scale there would be a significant number of species with an ambiguous moral status.

On this criterion, the obligations of the first precept would not apply in the case of microscopic forms of life such as viruses and bacteria, since these entities do not reincarnate and are simply functioning parts of an integral being rather than autonomous agents. A virus, for example, is not sentient (it lacks a central nervous system through which pain is experienced), it has no karmic history (it has not lived before), and being merely part of a larger organic whole has no more moral status than an arm or a leg. An implication of adopting the criterion of karmic life, however, is that the greater part of the natural world—especially inanimate nature such as mountains, rivers, and lakes—would lack inherent moral value, although retaining instrumental value to the extent that it provides support for karmic life.

Even though a natural hierarchy seems to exist, Buddhist literature does not make use of this structure to discuss matters such as species or selective conservation, which are issues that must be dealt with in modern ecology. The Buddha was certainly aware of the diversity of the animal world, stating, 'I do not see any other order of living beings as diverse as those of the animal kingdom' (S.iii.152). Nonetheless, while animals were classified in various ways (such as legless, two-legged, four-legged, or multi-legged) (A.v.21) and by mode of birth (such as from a womb or an egg) (S.iii.240) there is no discussion of a hierarchy within the animal kingdom itself or among the plant and animal kingdoms. This makes it difficult to address questions concerning conservation priorities. The authoritative 4th-century CE commentator Buddhaghosa, whose views we will have occasion to consider in the following chapters, suggests at one point that the larger the animal, the greater the 'demerit' in killing it (MA.i.189). On this understanding, killing an elephant is more serious than killing a fly on account of the greater effort required. However, this logic is not terribly helpful as a basis for the preservation of species, for sometimes it is more important to ensure the survival of endangered smaller species against their larger predators.

The practice of conservation can also lead to a conflict with *ahiṃsā*. For example, would Buddhism approve of a conservation measure that required the culling of some animals, even if such killing were ultimately to preserve the balance of the natural world? The Mahāyāna answer to this might introduce the concept of skilful means (*upāya-kauśalya*). As we saw in Chapter 1, skilful means allows the precepts to be relaxed or broken to varying degrees by a bodhisattva when done selflessly and for the welfare and happiness of other beings. However, applying skilful means with reference to the environment is a complicated issue and raises prior questions of the kind identified above, such as *why* the welfare of some species is to be considered more important than others on Buddhist principles.

Even the practice of 'releasing life' (*fang sheng*) referred to earlier has come in for criticism from animal rights groups. According to the Humane Society International, the practice involves the capture of hundreds of millions of animals worldwide, wreaking havoc on local ecosystems. The animals are often released in unsuitable conditions and die (or are recaptured) soon afterwards. In 2015, followers of the Taiwanese Buddhist master Hai Tao released hundreds of alien lobsters and crabs into the sea off Brighton in the UK causing untold damage to marine life. Those responsible were fined heavily and ordered to pay compensation.

Vegetarianism

Vegetarianism is an often-debated issue in environmental literature, and two arguments are frequently mentioned in its favour. First, modern ways of meat acquisition are uneconomic, wasteful, and harmful to the environment. Animals reared for their meat consume far greater resources than they yield, and animal agriculture also contributes to greenhouse gas emissions. Second, animals suffer when they are killed. This is known as the 'humane' argument and its aim is to reduce and ultimately put an end to animal suffering.

Among early texts, the *Jīvaka Sutta* of the *Majjhima Nikāya* sheds some light on the question of vegetarianism, even though there are no specific injunctions affirming or prohibiting it. The *sutta* describes various actions performed in the slaughter of an animal and each of these is seen as an evil deed deserving of demerit. These include the orders to fetch the being that is to be slaughtered, the act of fetching, the order for the being to be slaughtered, the act of slaughtering (which can cause immense pain), and the meat generated being served to a Buddha or disciple who eats it unknowingly. This discussion not only stresses that an animal is not to be killed in order to feed a monk, it also draws attention to the inhumane process of slaughter. Thus, the text appears to promote the humane argument for vegetarianism.

The suspicion that vegetarianism may have been a preferred choice is supported by the emphasis on non-violence and compassion, and the prohibition on the professions of hunters and butchers. It is important, at the same time, to note that in the *Jīvaka Sutta* the Buddha allowed monks to accept and eat the meat that was offered to them on their alms rounds if it was 'pure in three respects', namely if the monks had not seen, heard, or suspected that the animal was killed for their sake. Meat-eating was the norm in the Buddha's day, and the earliest sources depict the Buddha as following a non-vegetarian diet and even resisting an attempt to make vegetarianism compulsory for monks (the three restrictions laid down in the *Jīvaka Sutta* may well represent a compromise on this point). The Buddha's final meal appears to have been a dish of pork (D.ii.127), although its precise nature is disputed. Many contemporary monks justify meat-eating by reference to the *Jīvaka Sutta*, although at best this shows that meat-eating is permitted, not that it is compulsory. The practice of vegetarianism, by contrast, is increasingly common among lay Buddhists who regard it as a morally superior diet.

Mahāyāna sources categorically denounce the eating of meat. The eighth chapter of the *Laṅkāvatāra Sūtra* is a good example of the various reasons often cited in support of vegetarianism by the Mahāyāna. These include that meat-eating causes terror to living beings, acts as a hindrance to liberation, and causes personal distress, such as producing bad dreams. An appeal is also made to the cycle of transmigration, such that the animal to be slaughtered may have been one's mother, father, or other relative in another lifetime. Further, the dead animal, as with any other dead body, has an offensive odour. The Sūtra also discusses the example of a meat-eating king whose excessive fondness and greed for meat made him resort to cannibalism. As a result, he was alienated from his relatives, his friends, and his people, and eventually had to abdicate.

Vegetarianism is just one of a range of issues that concern the treatment of animals. Another is animal experimentation, a recent example of which is the use of dogs in gene-editing experiments. This has shown promising results in halting the development of Duchenne muscular dystrophy in both animals and humans. More controversial is the practice of vivisection. Vivisection has come to symbolize unnecessary cruelty to animals and a disregard for their suffering. Since, as mentioned above, Buddhism is a champion of compassion and non-violence, cruel and painful animal experimentation would be unacceptable. But this issue is not as simple as it appears, especially if the value given to other species is not egalitarian but relative. Considerable suffering results in the process of domesticating elephants, yet Buddhist texts turn a blind eye to such practices, except for certain rare examples such as the *Dubbalakattha Jātaka* (J.i.414–16) in which, though the pain is acknowledged, no directive to stop it is issued. This suggests that causing limited suffering to animals for human benefit may be tolerated.

Similar conflicts arise in the case of pest control. Would a farmer who uses pesticides in order to raise a healthy crop be acting immorally given the relativity of value among humans and other species? Clearly it would be better if pesticides were not needed, but if their use produces a larger crop which feeds more human beings, one can see an argument for employing them. The Vinaya, however, allows no latitude in this respect: monks and nuns were advised that if harmful insects or animals like venomous snakes entered their dwellings, they should be gently chased away rather than killed.

Towards a Buddhist ecology

The above discussion shows that it is not easy to classify Buddhism as categorically 'ecologically friendly'. Buddhist attitudes towards the natural world are complex and at times contradictory. On the one hand, references to plants and animals prove Buddhism's awareness of the world of nature. On the other, the importance given to human beings as well as the fact that ultimate value is given to the pursuit of liberation leaves a clear impression that the natural world has at best a secondary or instrumental value. When all is said and done, the aim of Buddhist teachings is not to redeem *saṃsāra* by restoring its ecological balance but to attain nirvana, or at least as a secondary goal, to pass from the human world to the relative security of a heavenly birth. The fact that the world is seen as inherently flawed and imperfect, and ultimately a disvalue, seems to cast a shadow over the prospects for a Buddhist ecology.

How does Buddhism compare with contemporary ecological movements such as 'deep ecology' and 'ecofeminism'? Although they have points in common, it is unlikely that the Buddhist perspective would coincide entirely with either of these. In contrast to deep ecology's goal of 'self–identification' (the process by which one develops an 'ecological Self'), Buddhism does not teach or encourage identification with nature. It acknowledges, in the principle of dependent origination, that certain causes lead to certain effects and that everything that exists is subject to this law. But this is not to claim a holistic connection between all things in the sense in which this is understood in deep ecology.

Some East Asian schools of Buddhism come close to such a view, but this is not how the concept of dependent origination is interpreted in mainstream Indian Buddhism. The view that the whole of the cosmos is intrinsically valuable and pure (often expressed in the image of 'Indra's net' referred to earlier) may even be problematic for ecology to the extent that it appears to place carbon dioxide gases and nuclear waste on a par with rivers and lakes. There are also differences with ecofeminism: not only does Buddhism not criticize (or even recognize) the concept of 'androcentricism' (the belief that it is the conduct of men rather than the conduct of all human beings that is responsible for the depleted state of the environment today), but it also contains many negative depictions of women and is considered by some to be misogynist.

Perhaps a better way of establishing a basis for ecology in Buddhism is to emphasize the ecological aspects of the virtues which are undeniably a central element in Buddhist teachings. Virtues such as compassion, non-violence, and wisdom promote ecological concern by their very nature. Even though such virtues were not originally taught for this reason, they do tend to promote

Box 6 Climate change

Climate science is a modern development, but the idea that climate change can have cataclysmic consequences is familiar in Buddhist mythology. The ancient sources teach that the universe evolves and declines over vast cycles of time and is periodically destroyed in turn by fire, flood, hurricanes, and earthquakes. It is also believed that such changes are driven by the collective karma of the world's inhabitants. From here it is only a short step to the modern belief that climate change is attributable to human behaviour.

In 2009 twenty-six Buddhist leaders from across the globe signed *A Buddhist Declaration on Climate Change* (updated in 2015), warning that failing to change current harmful trends involves a violation of the first precept (not to cause harm to living beings) 'on the largest possible scale'. While Buddhist virtues like frugality and mindfulness will by their nature reduce one's carbon footprint, the declaration pointed out that change is also required at a systemic level, such as the large-scale adoption of renewable sources of energy and new sources of transportation. Engaged Buddhists are active in supporting developments of this kind. As noted, blame for environmental degradation is often laid at the door of the West and its exploitative attitude towards nature, while Asian philosophies are thought to show greater respect for the environment. Ironically, however, Asian countries like China and India are today among the world's top polluters, and the most polluted urban areas are also to be found on the Asian continent.

an outlook and way of life that has much in common with the aims of the ecology movement. If so, it may be claimed that ecological concern is an implicit part of Buddhism's teachings and that by adhering to its ethical injunctions a person simultaneously lives in harmony with the environment.

Such an approach, however, provides only the beginnings of a Buddhist ecology and by itself is insufficient to bring about the structural change required to stave off ecological disaster (see Box 6). Nor does it provide a decision procedure for resolving difficult cases, such as where the building of a dam will provide electricity for isolated towns and villages at the cost of destroying the natural habitat of plants and animals. The basis upon which Buddhism would construct such a calculus has yet to be established.

Chapter 4
Sexuality and gender

Sexuality is another area on which Buddhism and Christianity seem at first glance to differ but on closer inspection—as in the case of ecology—turn out to have more in common than might at first be supposed. Christianity is sometimes seen as having a 'hang-up' about sex and to be overly concerned with virginity and celibacy, whereas Buddhism is perceived to be more relaxed and less 'neurotic' about this subject. The erotic art of India and Tibet and a plethora of popular books about Tantric sex reinforce the impression that Buddhism has a more 'liberated' view of sexual ethics.

Westerners who turn to Buddhism in the hope of finding the endorsement of a hippy-like attitude to 'free love' and 'polyamory', however, are likely to be disappointed. Contrary to popular belief, Buddhism is generally conservative on sexual matters, and traditional Buddhist societies tend to be reserved and even prudish where sex is concerned. Most Buddhist monks would be embarrassed to discuss questions of sex and reproduction, especially in the presence of women, and although attitudes are slowly changing, such matters are generally taboo. The Vinaya (iii.130) contains a rule that forbids monks speaking to women about obscene or erotic matters, and it may be thought that a frank discussion of sexual issues is sailing close to the wind. Although Tantric schools have flourished on and off down the centuries, the erotic art they made use of was mainly a symbolic means of conveying philosophical and religious teachings rather than for use in sexual rites. Even then, such ideas represent only a minor—if colourful—strand within the history of Buddhism as a whole.

It may be helpful to explore Christian attitudes to sex as an initial point of departure. Although attitudes have changed in modern times and Christians today have differing views, a basic feature of traditional Christian thought has been that sex should be closely linked to procreation, and that procreation is good and desirable. In the Old Testament, God expresses the desire that his creatures should 'be fruitful and multiply' (Genesis 1:22). The production of progeny is valued, and to remain unmarried was shameful in the eyes of the Old Testament (a similar attitude is evident in ancient Indian society). In the creation of progeny, parents were seen as playing their part in God's overall plan for creation. Although God is the ultimate author of life, through their union parents cooperate with him in the transmission of this divine gift. So important is this role that the institution that provides the social and legal framework for it, namely marriage, is given sacramental status and celebrated in church.

Buddhist reflections on sexuality have a different starting point, and its position is often characterized by scholars as 'antinatalist'. Buddhist teachings impose no obligation to procreate, and rather than a sign of divine bounty, Buddhist doctrine sees birth as the gateway to another round of suffering (*duḥkha*) in the cycle of *saṃsāra*. The generation of a new life is not seen in Buddhist teachings as confirmation that one is playing one's part in the unfolding of a divine plan, but as evidence of a failure to attain nirvana. As Buddhist scholar Amy Langenberg describes it, sexuality is the 'biological engine that turns the wheel of *saṃsāra*, fueling the cycle of human rebirth'.

Yet, balancing this, there is a more positive perspective that sees birth as an occasion for optimism. The birth of a child is normally a happy event, and Buddhists celebrate birthdays like everyone else. As noted in Chapter 3, to achieve what the texts call a 'precious human rebirth' is considered a great blessing, since according to traditional teachings rebirth as a human being provides the most favourable opportunity to attain nirvana. Furthermore, rebirth need not be seen as a futile series of endless cycles and can be conceptualized instead as an ascending spiral: in this way, despite being reborn, some ground has been gained and the goal of nirvana is closer than it was before. Finally, as we shall see, the normative Buddhist understanding of sexuality is procreative, a fact not easily reconcilable with the claim that Buddhism is antinatalist.

The dangers of sexual desire

Buddhism in general adopts a wary attitude towards sex. As an ascetic tradition it teaches that control of the appetites and desires is a prerequisite for spiritual development (similar ideas are also found in Christianity). The Second Noble Truth states that the cause of suffering is desire or craving (*tṛṣṇā*). Erotic desires are among the strongest, and represent a potent obstacle in the quest for liberation. The Buddha said that he knew of nothing that overpowers a man's mind so much as 'the form of a woman' (A.iii.68f). Perhaps this was behind his oft-quoted advice to his personal attendant Ānanda on how monks should behave towards women.

> Lord, how should we behave towards women?
>
> —Do not see them, Ānanda.
>
> But if we see them, how should we behave, Lord?
>
> —Do not speak to them, Ānanda.
>
> But if they speak to us, Lord, how should we behave?
>
> —Practise mindfulness, Ānanda.

(D.ii.141, trans. Walshe)

While such advice may be seen as simple misogyny, it also acknowledges the danger posed by sexual desire to members of a celibate community. Monks would come into daily contact with women in the villages as they received food on their alms round, and the Buddha was well aware how easily attraction could arise. He makes similar points about female sexual desire too, warning of the dangers of the desire women feel for men. Although women are said to be 'a snare of Māra' (the Buddhist devil), it is not basically women who are the problem, nor men, but the sexual desire that binds both to *saṃsāra*.

Marriage

While lay Buddhists are free to marry and have families, there is a clear sense in Buddhism that the lay estate is inferior to the monastic one and is a concession to those who are not yet able to sever the ties that bind them to the mundane world. This is reminiscent of the advice of St Paul that although a life of chastity is superior, 'it is better to marry than be aflame with passion' (1 Corinthians 7:9). Although there are exceptions, most notably in Japan where it is common for clergy to marry, the Buddhist ideal has always been to abandon family life and live either alone or in a celibate community (some believe the institution of monasticism originated with Buddhism and later spread to the West). As a candidate for such a community the Buddha provides the perfect role model: at the age of 29 he left the family home and remained celibate for the rest of his days. This does not mean, however, that he became an asexual or androgynous being, and John Powers has drawn attention to many textual sources that depict the Buddha as manly and attractive.

In Buddhism marriage is essentially a secular contract in which the partners assume obligations towards one another. Marriage is not a sacrament, and monks do not officiate at wedding ceremonies. Monks are also prohibited by the Vinaya from playing the role of matchmaker or go-between in bringing couples together. Nevertheless, it is customary for newlyweds to attend the local monastery for a blessing. The various forms of marriage arrangements found among Buddhists are determined more by local custom than Buddhist teachings, and such matters are essentially the responsibility of the secular authorities.

While monogamy is the preferred and predominant model, there is much local variation in marriage patterns across the Buddhist world. Early texts mention a variety of temporary and permanent arrangements entered into for both emotional and economic reasons, and in different parts of Buddhist Asia both polygamy and polyandry have been (and still are) practised. Early sources like the *Vimānavatthu* ('Stories of Heavenly Mansions') describe the challenges faced by the partners (particularly wives) in making a success of marriage, as well as pointing out the opportunities for merit-making such challenges present.

While as noted there is no 'official' Buddhist marriage service, some Western Buddhists have developed their own by adapting elements from the Christian service. These include same-sex marriages, the first of which were performed at the Buddhist Church of San Francisco in the early 1970s. Since Buddhism does not regard marriage as primarily a religious matter, it has no objection to divorce, but due to social pressures this is somewhat less common in Asian societies than in the West.

The third precept

The sexual morality of the laity is governed primarily by the third precept (Box 7). This precept prohibits 'misconduct' (*micchācāra*) in 'things sexual' (*kāmesu*). The wording of the precept is imprecise, and does not define which forms of behaviour constitute 'misconduct'. Although it makes no explicit reference to 'coveting another man's wife', as does the Third Commandment, the third precept is almost universally interpreted in Buddhist societies to prohibit, first and foremost, adultery. Little is said

Box 7 Ways in which the third precept can be broken, according to the ancient commentators

From the *Abhidharmakośa-bhāṣya* IV.74a–b (4th century CE):

1. Intercourse with a forbidden woman, that is, the wife of another, one's mother, one's daughter, or one's paternal or maternal relations

2. Intercourse with one's own wife through a forbidden orifice

3. In an unsuitable place: an uncovered spot, a shrine, or forest

4. At an unsuitable time: when the wife is pregnant, when she is nursing, or when she has taken a vow

From *The Jewel Ornament of Liberation* by sGam Po Pa (1079–1153):

1. In an improper part of the body, such as 'by way of the mouth or anus'

2. In an improper place, such as near the retinue of a guru, a monastery, a funeral monument (*stūpa*), or where many people have gathered

3. At an improper time, such as 'with a woman who has taken a vow, is pregnant or nursing a child, or in daylight'

4. Too often, for example 'more than five successive times'

5. In a generally improper way, such as by coercion, or with a man.

Similar injunctions are repeated in other authoritative sources, for example *The Sūtra on Lay Precepts* (*Upāsakaśīla-sūtra*) translated into Chinese in the 5th century CE, and Tsongkhapa's *Great Treatise on the Stages of the Path to Enlightenment* (*Lamrim Chenmo*) completed in Tibet in 1402.

about premarital sex, but the impression is given that marriage is the most appropriate forum for sexual intimacy. Some early

sources specify certain classes of women who are precluded as
sexual partners, such as close relatives and vulnerable young girls,
and medieval commentators expand on this by including
prohibited times, places, and methods of intercourse.

Apart from the third precept, other more general moral teachings
also have a bearing on sexual behaviour. For example, the
principle of *ahiṃsā* would require that one should not
intentionally harm another person physically or emotionally, thus
precluding rape, paedophilia, sexual harassment, and incest
(Box 8). Furthermore, all relationships should be informed by the
virtues of loving-kindness (*mettā*) and compassion (*karuṇā*). The
'Golden Rule' counsels that you should do nothing to others you
would not like done to yourself. This is specifically applied to
adultery, and it is said that just as you would not like another to
commit adultery with your wife, you should not do it with another
man's wife (S.v.354). Furthermore, the *śīla* component of the
Eightfold Path relating to Right Speech, Right Action, and Right
Livelihood would impose certain general restraints upon conduct,
such as a requirement to speak the truth and be straightforward
and honest in relationships, thereby avoiding the lies and deceit
common in extramarital affairs.

Homosexuality

The issue of homosexuality has provoked heated debate between
liberals and traditionalists in many religious communities. In
Buddhism, while there has been ample discussion of the matter,
tensions have not surfaced to the extent of threatening a schism as
they have, for example, within the Anglican churches. The Buddha
himself never passes judgement on the moral status of
homosexual acts, and in early sources homosexuality is not
discussed as a moral issue. Later commentators, however, express
disapproval of same-sex relationships. In his commentary,
Buddhaghosa speaks of the attraction of 'men for men' and
'women for women' as an example of decadence and moral decline

Box 8 Sex abuse scandals

A number of Buddhist communities have been shaken by sexual abuse scandals. To mention only recent examples from the USA (there have been many more in Asia and elsewhere), reports surfaced in 2014 that Zen master Joshu Sasaki Roshi of the Rinzai-ji Zen Center in Los Angeles was responsible for the abuse of hundreds of students. In 2017 accusations were made against a Tibetan lama, Norlha Rinpoche, founder of the Thubten Choling monastery in New York, alleging sexual relationships with students over decades. Around the same time, allegations of sexual impropriety at the Against the Stream Meditation Society in California resulted in the resignation of its founder, Noah Levine. Levine denied the allegations but many of the organization's centres have since closed down or changed their name.

Perhaps the most notorious case is that of Tibetan lama Sogyal Lakar Rinpoche, founder of the Rigpa community and author of the bestselling *The Tibetan Book of Living and Dying*. In July 2017 eight long-term students accused the then 70-year-old lama (who died in 2019) of sexual, physical, and psychological abuse spanning several decades. Soon afterwards, in 2018, a group called The Buddhist Project Sunshine issued a series of reports containing stories of abuse in Shambhala, an international group that follows the lama's teachings. These included allegations of sexual assault by the lama's son and spiritual heir Sakyong Mipham Rinpoche. Rigpa's international board issued a statement in September 2018 saying, 'we feel deeply sorry and apologise for the hurt experienced by past and present members'. It promised to disassociate itself from Sogyal and remove those in leadership positions tainted by the scandal. In the past teachers have attempted to pass off their aberrant behaviour as a form of 'crazy wisdom', but this is no longer seen as a credible excuse.

(DA.853), yet same-sex attraction per se is not generally what the texts condemn.

Homosexuality becomes problematic mainly in connection with admission to the Order. Certain types of people were not allowed to be ordained as monks, among them hermaphrodites and a class of individuals known in the Pali texts as *paṇḍakas*. It is not entirely clear who or what these were, but Peter Harvey concludes that the term denotes a type of 'sexually dysfunctional passive homosexual' male. Leonard Zwilling suggests that *paṇḍakas* were 'a socially stigmatised class of passive, probably transvestite, homosexuals' while Cabezón, in the most exhaustive study of Buddhist sexuality to date, translates the term as 'queer person'.

An alternative suggestion is that the association of *paṇḍakas* with homosexuality is a red herring, and that *paṇḍakas* were simply a class of males who suffered from a reproductive disorder involving the inability to produce or emit semen. However we understand the term, *paṇḍakas* as a group were excluded from ordination by the Buddha following an incident of lewd conduct by one of their number (Vin.i.85f.). In taking this decision, the Buddha's primary concern seems to have been to protect the reputation of the Order with the public at large, and there was no bar on the admission of non-practising homosexuals who did nothing to draw attention to their sexual orientation.

For those admitted to the monastic order, any kind of sexual activity—whether of a heterosexual or homosexual nature—is prohibited, and there are severe penalties for those who break the rules. Sexual intercourse is the first of the four most serious monastic offences (*vinaya-dharma*), and any monk or nun found guilty faces the penalty of permanent loss of communion with his fellow monks. More minor offences, such as masturbation or lewd conduct, of which many cases are reported in the Vinaya, are punished less severely.

The presence of gay monks in the Buddhist Order, however, has sometimes been a source of controversy. In July 2003 Phra Pisarn Thammapatee, one of Thailand's most famed monks, claimed there were about 1,000 gays among the country's 300,000 monks, an estimate others say is far too low. Whatever the actual number, he called for them to be expelled and for stricter screening of candidates for ordination. Expressing the view that those with 'sexual deviation' must be prevented from donning the saffron robes, he alleged that 'some homosexual monks have caused trouble in the temples'. Anti-gay rhetoric was also common in Asian countries as the HIV/AIDS pandemic developed through the 1980s.

In the course of the 1990s, the Dalai Lama made a number of statements on sexual ethics in his writings and in public meetings that caused concern to members of the LGBTQ community in North America. Community leaders in the San Francisco area asked for a meeting to clarify his views, and this took place in San Francisco in June 1997. In discussions the Dalai Lama affirmed the dignity and rights of gays and lesbians but stated that masturbation and oral or anal intercourse are improper activities and are proscribed for Buddhist practitioners.

Referring to authoritative texts of the kind cited earlier, the Dalai Lama stated that only the vagina should be used for sexual intercourse. He suggested that the purpose of sexuality as seen in India at the time was reproduction, which would explain why all sexual activity that cannot result in reproduction is proscribed. He himself stated, 'I think, basically, the purpose of sex is reproduction' (*World Tibet News*, 12 August 1997), and, as Janet Gyatso notes, Buddhism takes relations between a male and a fertile young woman as 'the gold standard for sex'. This seems to be the normative understanding of the high tradition as expressed through the pens of learned commentators who seek to exclude sexual practices that are non-procreative. The justification for this is never made explicit but such practices were presumably seen as contrary to Dharma in some way, or perhaps their disapproval was such a pervasive feature of the surrounding cultures that their rejection called for little justification.

Some Buddhists argue that if prohibitions of the kind described were merely the product of historical conditions and local custom they can safely be ignored by contemporary practitioners. The Dalai Lama has pointed out that Buddhist precepts take into account the time, culture, and society in which they originate. 'If homosexuality is part of accepted norms', he suggested, 'it is possible that it would be acceptable.' 'However,' he went on, 'no single person or teacher can redefine precepts. I do not have the authority to redefine these precepts since no one can make a unilateral decision or issue a decree.' In subsequent comments in 2014 the Dalai Lama commented that gay marriage is 'OK' and essentially a secular matter. He suggested that the prohibition on homosexual acts applies only to those who have taken the Buddhist precepts, and not to persons of other religions or none. However, he added that it is better for a Buddhist practitioner to engage in proscribed sexual activities if suppression of such desires would have more negative consequences, such as aggression or violence due to frustration. Other Tibetan teachers, meanwhile, have spoken more affirmatively about gay and lesbian relationships.

Historically, the Buddhist approach to non-standard genders (Box 9) and sexual practices has been one of 'tolerance yet unacceptance'. While not overtly hostile to those with a non-normative gender identity the monastic tradition seems based around a heteronormative imperative, a stance Buddhist feminists like Rita Gross (1993) have characterized as androcentric and patriarchal. Certainly, there is little discussion in the sources of sexual ethics for women. There have been times when same-sex relationships were celebrated in Buddhist cultures. For example, the *Nanshoku Okagami* ('the Great Mirror of Male Love') is a collection of Japanese homoerotic Buddhist stories published

Box 9 Transgenderism

According to contemporary estimates, up to 2 per cent of the population are born with intersex characteristics (lower estimates are also found depending on how these characteristics are defined). Classical Buddhist sources hold that gender can change from one life to another, and whether one is born male, female, or hermaphrodite is due to the effect of karma from previous lives. There are also stories in the early sources of bodies changing gender within the same lifetime, such that due to karmic factors men become women and vice versa (Vin.iii.35), and some Buddhists explain homosexuality as the result of a past gender reasserting itself in the present life. Such changes, however, were not seen as a hindrance to spiritual progress, which is Buddhism's primary concern.

The bodhisattva Avalokiteśvara mentioned in Chapter 1 (see Figure 2) takes on a feminine aspect in Indo-Tibetan Buddhism as the savioures Tārā, and in east Asia changes gender completely to become Guanyin. Sexual orientation and gender were thus regarded as somewhat fluid, and not in themselves morally problematic, although those with an intersex identity were seen as vulnerable to the carnal lusts of both sexes making religious progress more difficult.

In Burma there are transvestite male ritual specialists known as *acault* who adopt stereotypical female behaviour following possession by the goddess Manguedon, and in Thailand the 'third gender' of kathoey (generally known as ladyboys) is well represented. In 2009, the winner of the transsexual 'Miss Tiffany Universe' beauty contest, Sorrawee 'Jazz' Nattee, was ordained as a monk in southern Thailand. Jazz had lived as a woman for most of her adult life and had received breast implants but had never undergone transgender surgery. A condition of ordination was that Jazz 'detransition' by removal of the implants, which in the eyes of the *saṅgha* restored his original male condition.

in 1687. Historically, however, Buddhism has had little interest in what today are known as LGBTQ issues, being concerned mainly to persuade people to become celibate and renounce what texts call the 'village practice' of sexual intercourse.

Although this chapter began by drawing a contrast between Buddhist and Christian views of sexuality and reproduction, we seem to have uncovered an unexpected area of agreement. If Buddhism is antinatalist, as many scholars suggest, it seems strange that it affirms only reproductive sex as legitimate. We can understand why Christians might see things this way given the biblical emphasis on procreation, but, as already noted, Buddhism begins from different premises. There is much that is unclear in Buddhist teachings on sexual ethics and many points that need to be more carefully explained or thought through. As traditional Buddhism encounters a hedonistic West where celibacy is not much in vogue and where self-identified communities with diverse sexual orientations and expressions are increasingly in evidence, this remains an important area for further investigation and dialogue.

Chapter 5
War, violence, and terrorism

The 20th century proved to be one of the bloodiest in history. Wars on a scale never seen caused untold destruction taking a toll of over 100 million lives. Sadly, the present century has also begun on a belligerent note. There have been wars in Iraq and Afghanistan, and bitter civil wars in Syria and Yemen. Terrorist attacks and random shootings have become almost routine events. The terrible events of 11 September 2001 in New York brought home to the world the damage that can be inflicted by well-trained and coordinated terrorists who act without fear for their lives. Europe has also suffered a spate of terrorist attacks, such as the Bataclan incident in Paris on 13 November 2015 in which attackers killed 130 people, and similar events have occurred elsewhere in the world.

Opinion about how best to respond to these violent events has been divided. In the aftermath of the attack on the World Trade Center, President Bush declared a 'war on terror'. Others saw the military response as a mistake, and protest marches were organized by pacifist groups including many Buddhist organizations. Is Buddhism categorically opposed to the use of force, or does it depend on the nature of the conflict? Can there be a 'just war' according to Buddhism, and what is the appropriate response in the face of terrorist outrages?

Classical sources on war

Buddhist teachings strongly oppose the use of violence, analysing it as the product of greed (*rāga*), hatred (*dveṣa*), and delusion (*moha*). The false belief in a self (*ātman*) and a desire to protect that self against 'others' who are thought to threaten it is seen as an underlying cause of aggression. Buddhism holds that drawing a sharp boundary between self and others leads to the construction of a self-image that sees all that is not of 'me and mine' (such as those of another country, race, or creed) as alien and threatening. When this strong sense of self is reduced by practising Buddhist teachings, such egocentric preoccupations are thought to subside and be replaced by a greater appreciation of the kinship among beings. This dissipates the fear and hostility which engender conflict and so removes one of the main causes of violent disputes. When threatened, Buddhists are encouraged to practise patience (*kṣānti*), and there are many stories of exemplary patience as well as practices designed to cultivate toleration and forbearance. Anger is seen as a negative emotion that serves only to inflame situations and inevitably rebounds with negative karmic consequences.

Early Buddhist literature contains numerous references to war. The view expressed almost unanimously in the texts is that since war involves killing, and killing is a breach of the first precept, it is morally wrong to fight in either offensive or defensive wars. In marked contrast to the teachings of the Qur'an, the Buddha states (Sn.iv.308–11) that warriors who die in battle go not to heaven but to a special hell, since at the moment of death their minds are intent on killing living beings. The 4th-century commentator Vasubandhu in his *Abhidharmakośa-bhāṣya* expresses the view that even a conscript is guilty of killing unless he firmly resolves not to kill anyone even to save his own life. The same text affirms that killing is bad karma even in the case of self-defence or when defending friends.

A legend in the commentary to the *Dhammapada* narrates how the Buddha's kinsmen, the Śākyas, offered only token resistance when attacked by King Viḍūḍabha, and allowed themselves to be slaughtered rather than break the precept against taking life. The *Jātakas* contain stories about princes and kings who were so horrified by violence that they renounced their kingdoms to become ascetics or refused to defend themselves in the face of attack. The example of the Emperor Aśoka in the 3rd century BCE is often given as the model for a Buddhist ruler. After a bloody campaign in the thirteenth year of his reign, Aśoka renounced violence and vowed henceforth to rule by Dharma. The edicts promulgated throughout his empire speak of tolerance and compassion and state that conquest by Dharma is preferable to conquest by force or coercion. Aśoka modelled himself on the classical ideal of the *Cakravartin*, the righteous Buddhist king. It is notable, however, that although the *Cakravartin* is portrayed as conquering peacefully through the power of Dharma, he nonetheless retains his army and is accompanied by it on his travels to neighbouring kingdoms. Aśoka, likewise, did not disband his army or abjure the use of force.

In light of such anomalies Buddhist scholar Steven Collins has detected 'two modes' of Dharma in the canon with respect to violence. In the first, 'the assessment of violence is context-dependent and negotiable', and in the second it is 'context-independent and non-negotiable'. The second mode represents the absolutist pacifist stance we have just been considering, while the first is based on the observation that on certain occasions the Buddha seems tacitly to allow—or at least does not explicitly condemn—the use of force by kings. A golden opportunity for him to do so occurred about a year before his death when the warmongering King Ajātasattu sent his chief minister to the Buddha seeking advice on his plan to attack the neighbouring Vajjis (D.ii.72ff.). Instead of delivering a forthright condemnation of the planned attack (perhaps a politically difficult option given the royal patronage the *saṅgha* enjoyed) the Buddha simply commented obliquely on seven positive features of Vajjian society.

Buddhism at war

The pacifist ideal of the classical sources (see Box 10) has not prevented Buddhists throughout Asia fighting battles and conducting military campaigns from a mixture of political and religious motives. As Michael Jerryson notes, 'In countries such as Korea, Tibet, China, Japan, and Thailand, Buddhist monasteries served as military outposts, monks led revolts, and Buddhist principles served as war rhetoric for heads of state.' Let us look at a few examples, beginning with south Asia.

The early history of Sri Lanka was convulsed by war between Sinhalese and Tamils, and King Duṭṭhāgamaṇi (1st century BCE) is regarded as a national hero for defeating the Tamil general Eḷāra who had invaded the island from south India. Duṭṭhāgamaṇi's victory was glorified in a famous chronicle known as the *Mahāvaṃsa* (5th–6th centuries CE) which relates that his army was accompanied by Buddhist monks and that Buddhist relics adorned the spears of the soldiers. Monks disrobed and joined the

Box 10 From the *Dhammapada* (trans. Norman)

'He abused me, he struck me, he overcame me, he robbed me.' Of those who do not wrap themselves up in it hatred is quenched. (v.3)

All tremble at violence; to all life is dear. Comparing (others) with oneself, one should not kill or cause to kill. (v.129)

Whoever, having laid aside violence with regard to creatures moving and still, neither kills nor causes to kill, him I call a brahman. (v.405).

army to fight in what the chronicle depicts as a 'holy war', although no such concept is legitimized in orthodox teachings. Despite this apparent endorsement by the *saṅgha*, after his victory Duṭṭhāgamaṇi (like Aśoka before him) felt remorse at the loss of life, whereupon, according to the chronicle, he was reassured by enlightened monks (*arhats*) that he was responsible for the deaths of just 'one and a half people'. The meaning of this cryptic remark seems to be that in contrast to Buddhists, Tamils counted only as half persons, since they were 'evil men of wrong views' little better than 'beasts'.

In modern times, leading Sinhalese monks such as the late Walpola Rahula have spoken with approval of 'religio-nationalism' and described Duṭṭhāgamaṇi's campaign as a 'crusade'. Contemporary supporters of Sinhalese nationalism include monks who believe that only the expulsion of non-Buddhist minorities from the country will bring a lasting peace. These monks have been inspired by an ideology known as 'Jathika Chintanaya' ('nationalist thought') which expresses its values in the slogan 'Raṭa, Jātiya, Āgama' ('country, race, and religion'). Buddhist organizations expressing such nationalist sentiments include the Bodu Bala Sena ('the army of Buddhist power'). Human rights abuses were widespread in the Sri Lankan civil war, and although hostilities ceased in 2009, harassment, intimidation, torture, exploitation, and violence by Buddhists have continued, including attacks on Muslim and Christian minorities.

Buddhists were inevitably caught up in the turbulent history of South-East Asia in the 20th century as Communist and Maoist movements fought for political power in Vietnam and Cambodia. The Khmer Rouge destroyed almost all of Cambodia's 3,600 Buddhist temples and reduced the number of monks from 50,000 to barely 3,000. The fear of Communist insurgency in Thailand led some monks to take a militant stand. In the 1970s the monk Kittivuḍḍho made a number of controversial public statements to the effect that killing Communists in defence of the Thai nation,

Buddhism, and the monarchy was a religious duty that justified the suspension of the ordinary rules of morality. He compared Communism to the devil Māra and spoke of the killing of Communists as an act of great merit. In a speech to soldiers he offered a utilitarian justification for his views, stating that killing 5,000 Communists in order to ensure the happiness of 42 million Thais was legitimate. The role of the CIA in fomenting Buddhist opposition to Communism in this period has been detailed by Eugene Ford.

Turning to north and east Asia we see again the involvement of monks in insurrections and military campaigns. This was most noticeable in Japan, where monasteries became wealthy land-owning institutions employing bands of warrior monks (*sōhei*) to provide protection and intimidate opponents. In the feudal conflicts of the medieval period, battles were fought between one sect and another and against military rulers (*shōgun*) and the imperial court. The teachings and practices of Zen Buddhism were found helpful by the military caste (*bushi*) as techniques to discipline the mind in battle and dispel the fear of death.

Martial arts such as swordsmanship and archery were influenced by Zen teachings, and the doctrine of emptiness (*śūnyatā*) helped provide justification both for taking life and contemplating the loss of one's own life with equanimity. In the final analysis, so the reasoning of teachers such as Takuan Sōhō Zenji (1573–1645) went, there is only emptiness or the void: life is like a dream and the one who strikes and the one who is struck are merely phantoms. The Mahāyāna teaching of 'skilful means' was invoked to justify the taking of life and other prohibited acts; the principle invoked was that compassion requires bodhisattvas to break the rules when some greater good is at stake.

In the modern period, Buddhist religious groups have had a close involvement with Japanese nationalism and militarism. The Zen and Pure Land denominations provided financial support for the 1937–1945 war with China, and in the Second World War most Buddhist schools supported the Japanese war effort against the Allies. In books such as *Zen at War*, Brian Victoria has exposed the extent to which many well-known Zen masters were enthusiastic advocates of war, to the surprise and embarrassment of their pacifist Western followers. The Zen master Harada Daiun Sōgaku (1871–1961) wrote, 'without plunging into the war arena, it is totally impossible to know the Buddha Dharma'. Yasutani Haku'un (1885–1973), well known in the West as one of the founders of the Sanbō Kyōdan school, expressed the following view on the ethics of killing in war:

> Of course one should kill, killing as many as possible. One should, fighting hard, kill everyone in the enemy army. The reason for this is that in order to carry compassion and filial obedience through to perfection it is necessary to assist good and punish evil. However, in killing one should swallow one's tears, bearing in mind the truth of killing yet not killing.

Such remarks about 'killing yet not killing' are typical of the sophistry Zen masters resorted to in their justification of war. In his second book *Zen War Stories*, Victoria cites many more examples of Buddhist militarism in Japan, and comments:

> In infusing the suicidal Japanese military spirit, especially when extended to civilians, with the power of religious belief, Japan's wartime Zen leaders revealed themselves to be *thoroughly and completely morally bankrupt*. [emphasis in original]

Belligerent tendencies of the above kind are perhaps inevitable if one holds the belief that all duality (including that between good and evil) must be transcended. As Winston King notes in his book *Zen and the Way of the Sword*, 'Zen...has no intrinsic ethical quality or inner monitor, but...historically seems to be primarily a psychological technique for maximizing the visceral energies whatever their orientation.' The leaders of Japan's main Zen sects issued a public apology for Zen's complicity in Japanese militarism in 2001, although they did not criticize specific teachers by name or repudiate their teachings affirming violence.

The militarism described above, however, is far from all-pervasive. In Japan, the Nipponzan Myōhōji sect founded in 1917 staunchly supports pacifism and opposes nuclear weapons. Monks from the group can often be seen on peace marches chanting and beating their drums. The Nipponzan Myōhōji has built over eighty 'Peace Pagodas' worldwide. The group hopes that the pagodas and the sacred relics they house will exert a calming influence on a troubled world. The Cambodian monk Mahā Ghosānanda was influenced by the ideals of this group. He worked as a consultant to the United Nations and became an ambassador for peace worldwide. Daisetsu Ikeda, president of Sōka Gakkai International (SGI), has also been an active peace campaigner for many years. The objectives of SGI include the aim of 'Working for peace by opposing all forms of violence and contributing to the welfare of humankind by pursuing humanistic culture and education'. Another Japanese group active on this front is the Risshō Kōsei-kai, which in 1978 established the Niwano Peace Foundation 'to contribute to the realization of world peace'.

In Tibet it is estimated that 6 million Tibetans died and a further million fled the country as refugees in the aftermath of the Chinese invasion in 1959. Despite a systematic and brutal programme to suppress Buddhism, the Dalai Lama, the *de facto* leader of Tibet's Buddhists, has followed a policy of non-violent resistance, in recognition of which he was awarded the Nobel Peace Prize in 1989.

The just war

The image of Buddhism as exclusively a peace-loving religion is clearly incomplete, and the facts set out above problematize the issue of war and peace from a Buddhist perspective. If all use of force is ruled out, as the early texts suggest, how will it be possible to restrain violent criminals or terrorists who threaten innocent citizens? Since no Buddhist country has abolished the rule of law or is without some means to enforce it (such as an army or police force), it seems that Buddhist moral principles must allow for some use of force if a stable society—itself a Buddhist ideal—is to be achieved. And if the use of force is morally justified against internal threats to security, might it not also be justified against external ones?

One of the earliest Western thinkers to ponder such questions was St Augustine (354–430 CE), and in the medieval period his ideas were developed and refined by St Thomas Aquinas (1224–74). Christian thinkers developed the doctrine of a 'just war' because of a perceived conflict between, on the one hand, the need to defend Christian communities and states against attack and, on the other, religious teachings such as the commandment against killing and the injunction to 'turn the other cheek' (Matthew 5:38–41). In modern times, interest in the concept of a just war has been heightened as moralists, politicians, and military strategists ponder dilemmas arising in connection with nuclear weapons, the need for humanitarian intervention in situations like Kosovo, and the use of drone strikes as part of the 'war on terror'.

Just war thinking has two main branches. The first concerns the conditions that need to be satisfied for going to war and is summed up in the Latin phrase *jus ad bellum* ('rightness in going to war'). The second, known as *jus in bello* ('rightness in the conduct of war'), concerns things it is legitimate and not legitimate to do once a military campaign has been initiated. The general consensus among theorists is that certain conditions need to be satisfied for war to be declared, such as it must be waged by a legitimate authority (normally a state) and can only be waged as a last resort. Two broad principles then govern the actual conduct of a military campaign: the violence used must be proportional to the injury suffered, and the weapons used must discriminate between combatants and non-combatants.

Traditional Buddhist commentators sometimes express views of a similar kind, but there is no systematic body of thought explaining how the pacifist ideal of *ahiṃsā* is to be accommodated to the realities of social and political life. As mentioned earlier, Buddhism has had from its inception a close relation with political authorities (some may think the relationship too close). As part of this relationship—envisaged as a partnership of the temporal and spiritual—Buddhist teachers offered advice on the principles that should guide rulers, modelled on the classical notion of the ideal king (*Cakravartin*). One authoritative example of such advice is *A Treatise on Ethics for Kings: An Ornament for Rulers* composed in 1895 by the great Tibetan scholar Mipham (1846–1912) (see Figure 5). According to its English translator, this 'is one of the longest classical works on the theory and practice of Buddhist kingship ever written in any Buddhist language'. The work was composed some two centuries after temporal and religious authority in Tibet were consolidated in the office of the Dalai Lama, a development which perhaps explains the need for a treatise of this kind.

In Mipham's view the king, as overseer of the law, should not hesitate to stamp out crime and improper behaviour by punishing evildoers. The failure to impose punishment, says Mipham, will lead to the increase of evil and the destruction of the kingdom. The punishment should be guided by five principles: it should be just, fitting, principled, moderate, and benevolent. It should also be proportionate to the crime and imposed only after a fair trial. While the punishment of wrongdoers could include 'putting them in chains, imprisoning them, beating them, threatening, harassing, or banishing them, or confiscating their wealth', it should not include the death penalty, the amputation of limbs, or other cruel or excessive punishments since these cannot be 'reversed or remedied' in the event of judicial error. In sum,

5. Mipham.

'Even though the king is compassionate,' says Mipham, 'he will impose timely and just punishments on criminals.'

Mipham also sets out certain rules of war involving three types of strategy. Initially, the righteous king tries to avoid war by seeking allies and using diplomatic strategies (such as enticements and threats). In the second, he reflects on ways to achieve victory with minimal loss of life. In the third, once conflict becomes inevitable, he marshals his forces employing appropriate military tactics. If he wounds or kills opponents in battle 'this constitutes only a minor moral fault' that may attract no karmic retribution 'because the motivating force behind his action was unwavering compassion'.

It can be seen that Mipham adopts a relatively robust position in the face of threats to the state from within and without. 'If someone else acts violently toward you for no reason,' he writes, 'do not back off, but rather stand firm.' He envisages a Spartan-like society where citizens play an active role in defence of the state. He writes: 'Strong armour and fortifications, and various types of horses and weaponry are amassed in the homes of every individual, each of whom is courageous and knows the martial arts.' Given this state of military readiness, 'Soldiers and generals clad in armour will, when needed, spring immediately to action without delay.' Despite this hawkish realpolitik we see the underlying tension with *ahiṃsā* resurface when Mipham tells us: 'All living creatures value their own lives, so the king must completely abandon killing... and to the best of his ability bring an end to violence against any being, down to birds and wild animals.' While this tension remains unresolved, we may agree with Stephen Jenkins that Buddhism finally arrived at the position that 'a measured and principled use of violence, governed by compassionate intentions, enhances security and serves the purposes of acquiring and retaining power, while maintaining moral integrity'.

Terrorism

'Terrorism' is not an easy term to define since, as commonly noted, one man's terrorist is another man's freedom fighter. Groups who are characterized as 'terrorist' today can tomorrow constitute the official government of a country, as in the case of the African

National Congress, which was designated as a terrorist organization by Britain and the United States in 1987 but subsequently came to form the government of South Africa. The term 'terrorist' was originally coined and applied in self-reference by French revolutionaries in the 1790s, but few people today would welcome the epithet, preferring to describe themselves as 'urban guerrillas' or even 'holy warriors'.

The Wordnet online dictionary at Princeton University defines terrorism as 'the calculated use of violence (or threat of violence) against civilians in order to attain goals that are political or religious or ideological in nature; this is done through intimidation or coercion or instilling fear'. This definition makes clear why terrorism is regarded as immoral in terms of just war theory: terrorist groups do not constitute a legitimate political authority (contrary to the *jus ad bellum* provisions) and they specifically target civilians in their attacks in order to spread terror among the population at large (contrary to the *jus in bello* requirements).

Contemporary Buddhist responses to terrorism have tended to make three main points. First, that we must try to understand fully the causes that have led to the present situation. The doctrine of dependent origination (*pratītya-samutpāda*) teaches that conflicts arise from a nexus of causes and conditions, and lasting solutions cannot be found until we fully understand the reasons why these situations come about. Second, we must respond to aggression with compassion as opposed to hatred; and third, violence will only lead to a cycle of retaliation and make the chances of peace even more remote. The need for reflection and self-criticism was mentioned by Thich Nhat Hanh. After the attacks on the World Trade Center 11 September 2001, he expressed the view that America would have been better off with dialogue. Identifying the key question as 'Why would anyone hate us enough to do that?', he offered the response: 'If we are able to listen, they will tell us.'

Aung San Suu Kyi, who at the time was leader of the Burmese democracy movement and winner of the 1991 Nobel Peace Prize, made the following comment on terrorism:

> You know, I am a Buddhist. As a Buddhist, the answer is very simple and clear. That is compassion and mercy is the real panacea. I am sure that, when we have compassion and mercy in our heart, we can overcome not only terrorism but also many other evil things that are plaguing the world.

Subsequent events, however, have given her words something of a hollow ring. Since becoming the *de facto* leader of Myanmar in 2016, Suu Kyi has been denounced by her former international supporters for refusing to condemn what has been described by the UN as 'a textbook example of ethnic cleansing' against the country's Rohingya Muslim minority. There were anti-Muslim riots in Myanmar in 2000–1 and 2011–12, and in 2017 the UN Secretary-General noted how 'A vicious cycle of persecution, discrimination, radicalization and violent repression has led more than 400,000 desperate people to flee' (the figure is now closer to 700,000). Investigators attribute the attacks to a combination of Buddhist fanaticism and Burmese nationalism and speak of an orchestrated campaign of 'Buddhist terrorism' against the Muslim minority.

The Burmese Ma Ba Tha ('The Association for Protection of Race and Religion') enjoys the support of many Buddhist clergy and has been at the forefront of anti-Muslim protests, citing fears about the threat of the higher Muslim birth rate to the survival of Buddhism (this despite the fact that Muslims constitute less than 5 per cent of the population). The group has successfully lobbied for laws restricting interfaith marriage. Ironically, many of its members participated peacefully in the 'Saffron Revolution' of 2007 in a non-violent attempt to overthrow military rule, taking the 'discourse on loving-kindness' (*Mettāsutta*) as their inspiration.

A less publicized campaign has also been under way against the largely Christian minority in Kachin state in the north. Civilians have been systematically targeted by the Burmese army, and some 130,000 people have been displaced over the past decade. Suu Kyi has offered no 'simple and clear' response to these problems, and there has been little mention of Buddhist 'compassion and mercy' in her public statements. Both she and her government have also faced criticism for prosecuting journalists and activists, and as a result many of the international honours she was awarded have been revoked.

The situation in Myanmar is not unique. Reference has already been made to human rights abuses by Buddhists in Sri Lanka, and in Japan and China Buddhism has often colluded with state institutions of repression and control. With respect to Japan, Brian Victoria has explored the role of Zen nationalist ideology in domestic terrorism. In the 1930s, Zen practitioner Inoue Nisshō was the self-confessed leader of a terrorist group responsible for two killings and several failed assassination attempts (the band planned to kill some twenty influential figures). Inoue's claim to have experienced *kenshō* ('seeing one's nature') was validated by one of the greatest Zen masters of the day, Yamamoto Gempō (1866–1961). Like many in the tradition, Inoue 'weaponized' Zen and harnessed it to an extreme right-wing ideology.

In sum, it seems that when confronting the issues of war and terrorism, Buddhists are pulled in two directions. On the one hand, the classical sources teach strict pacifism, while on the other Buddhist states have not been averse to the use of force and have frequently invoked religion as a justification for military campaigns. In south Asia this tension was relieved to some degree by subsequent merit-making activities, such as making lavish donations to the Order following a military victory. In Japan and other parts of east Asia the dissonance seems to have been less troubling. Perhaps it should be noted that war has rarely—if ever—been used by Buddhists for purposes of religious coercion.

Instead, as Jerryson points out, 'Most Buddhist-inspired wars are either the result of a closely-aligned monasticism and state, or a movement that contains millenarian elements.' In modern times much violence has resulted from an explosive mixture of religion, ethnicity, and nationalism and shows little sign of abating.

While pacifism remains the ideal, and may be a viable option for those who have renounced the world, pragmatic commentators like Mipham clearly do not see it as a workable social policy. Mipham allows the use of force in the punishment of criminals, and it is not hard to see how the same principle could be used to justify a defensive war. The argument would be that those who seek to subvert or overthrow a just social order—from either within or without—deserve punishment. Of course, any reasonable person would do well to pay heed to the three points made earlier by Buddhists, namely the importance of seeking to understand the causes of a conflict, showing compassion to opponents, and endeavouring to resolve disputes by peaceful means. It has been wisely said that 'pacifism does not mean passivism', and there is much useful work that can be done to remove injustice and the causes of dissent before they erupt into violent conflict.

Chapter 6
Abortion

How do Buddhist ethical teachings like *ahiṃsā* affect its approach to abortion? Is Buddhism 'pro-life' or 'pro-choice'? The Buddhist belief in rebirth clearly introduces a new dimension to the abortion debate. For one thing, it puts the question 'When does life begin?' in an entirely new light. For Buddhism, life is a continuum with no discernible starting point, and birth and death are like a revolving door through which an individual passes again and again. But does belief in rebirth increase or reduce the seriousness of abortion? It may be thought that it reduces it, since all that has been done is to postpone rebirth to a later time—the child that was to have been born simply arrives later. This argument, however, would also legitimize the killing of adults, since they too will be born again. Instead, the first precept is widely understood as prohibiting the intentional killing of a human being at any stage of life.

Buddhist embryology

The Buddha divided the stages of childbearing into four: the fertile period, pregnancy, birth, and nursing (M.ii.148). In keeping with traditional Indian medical thought, he explained conception as a natural process that occurs when three specific conditions are fulfilled (M.i.256). On this understanding, (i) intercourse must take place (ii) during the woman's fertile period, and (iii) there must be available the consciousness of a deceased person (known as a *gandharva*) seeking rebirth.

Early Buddhists shared the beliefs of the ancient Indian medical tradition known as Āyurveda regarding the reproductive process. On this understanding, when intercourse takes place, the semen mingles with the residue of menstrual blood, and if a *gandharva* is available it 'descends' into the union of these fluids—this is 'conception'. The sex of the individual was thought to be determined at this time (although in exceptional cases it could change during life, as we have seen) and from conception onwards the spiritual and material components that constitute the new individual—what Buddhists call *nāma-rūpa* (mind and body)—evolve together and remain united 'like a mixture of milk and water' until they once again separate at death.

Once consciousness has 'descended' into the womb and conception has occurred, the embryo develops through a set number of stages. In *The Path of Purification* (236), the commentator Buddhaghosa lists four stages of the early embryo during the first month after conception. The first stage is the *kalala*, in which the tiny embryo is described as 'clear and translucent' and likened to 'a drop of purest oil on the tip of a hair'. The following three stages are the *abudda*, the *pesi*, and the *ghana*, terms that connote increasing density and solidity. The stages of embryonic development are summarized in an 18th-century Tibetan treatise entitled *The Lamp Thoroughly Illuminating the Presentation of the Three Basic Bodies*. This confirms that the early views remained influential and underwent little modification. The text narrates the course of development within the first twenty-eight days of life:

> When the oval-shaped foetus has passed seven days ... [it] becomes viscous both outside and inside, like yogurt, but has not become flesh. When another seven days pass ... the foetus becomes fleshy but cannot withstand pressure. After another seven days it hardens ... [so that] the flesh is now hard and can bear pressure.

When this, in turn, has passed seven days... the foetus develops legs
and arms, in the sense that five protuberances—signs of the two
thighs, two shoulders and head—stand out clearly.

The sources cited by this text are in broad agreement that the
length of a normal pregnancy is 38 weeks: one source places it at
268 days and another at 270 days. Modern estimates calculate the
average length of pregnancy as 280 days from the onset of the last
menstrual period.

Abortion and the precepts

Interpreting the traditional teachings in the light of modern
scientific discoveries, the most common view among Buddhists
today, particularly those from traditional countries, is that
fertilization is the point at which individual human life
commences. As a consequence, abortion is widely seen as contrary
to the first precept. As already noted, the precept prohibits
causing harm to anything which has *prāṇa*, which literally means
'breath'. Because a foetus does not breathe, it could be argued that
it does not fall within the scope of the precept. The meaning of
prāṇa, however, is not restricted to respiration and has the more
general sense of a life force or vital energy that flows through the
body. Since *prāṇa* is present throughout all stages of foetal life
(were it not, the foetus would not develop) it is difficult to argue
that the moral protection of the first precept does not apply to the
unborn. This also makes it difficult to draw lines at certain stages
of foetal development in order to establish a point up to which
abortion may be allowed.

Any ambiguity there may be thought to be in the first precept with
respect to abortion is removed in the equivalent precept in the
Vinaya (the third *pārājika*) which prohibits taking a human life
(*manussa-viggaha*). One formulation of the precept (Box 11)
explicitly mentions abortion, and the commentary explains that
the prohibition applies from the moment of conception. Although

> ## Box 11 The third *pārājika*, the monastic precept against taking human life
>
> An ordained monk should not intentionally deprive a living thing of life even if it is only an ant. A monk who deliberately deprives a human being of life, even to the extent of causing an abortion, is no longer a follower of the Buddha. As a flat stone broken asunder cannot be put back together again, a monk who deliberately deprives a human being of life is no longer a follower of the Buddha.
>
> (Vin.i.97)

this precept applies only to monks and nuns, it confirms that life was thought to begin at conception rather than some later point.

Despite the condemnation of abortion, the case histories recorded in the Vinaya disclose that as medical practitioners, monks sometimes became involved in procuring and performing abortions. Monks frequently acted as counsellors and were sometimes drawn into the kinds of problems that arise in family life, such as an unwanted pregnancy. The motives reported in the sources for seeking an abortion include concealing extramarital affairs, as when a married woman becomes pregnant by her lover; seeking to prevent an inheritance by aborting the heir prior to birth; and in situations of domestic rivalry between co-wives as when one wife produces progeny and another does not. In cases of this kind, monks sometimes brought their medical knowledge to bear in an attempt to cause a miscarriage. The methods used included ointments, potions, and charms, pressing or crushing the womb, and scorching or heating it. Monks who were involved in performing or procuring abortions were expelled from communion with their fellow monks for life, the severest sanction available.

Beyond the texts of monastic law, more popular literature describes the evil karmic consequences of abortion, sometimes in lurid detail. Stories in the *Dhammapada* commentary, the *Petavatthu* ('Stories of the Departed'), and the *Jātakas* (such as the *Saṃkicca Jātaka*) narrate the evil consequences which follow an abortion, such as the loss of offspring in future lives, acts of revenge, and rebirth in hell. At both a popular and scholarly level, therefore, the early teachings are consistent in depicting abortion as an immoral act that brings karmic suffering in its wake.

Personhood

Much of the philosophical discussion of abortion in the West has focused on the criterion of moral personhood and the point at which a foetus acquires the capacities that entitle it to moral respect. The philosophical foundations for this approach were laid by Locke and Kant, who argued that only rational beings are 'persons' with moral status. For them, the paradigm moral subject is the adult in possession of her intellectual faculties.

Locke and Kant did not apply these conclusions to abortion, but building on their views contemporary philosophers who take a liberal position on abortion argue that what we value is not human life *per se*, in the biological sense, but rather the higher faculties and powers human beings possess, such as reason, self-consciousness, autonomy, the capacity to form relationships, and similar abilities. When these faculties are present, they say, we can speak of a moral 'person', and when they are absent there is only biological life. On this reasoning, before it acquires these attributes a foetus is only a 'potential person' rather than an actual one, and so does not have a claim to full moral status and the right to life that entails.

As an example of this approach, contemporary feminist writers such as Mary Anne Warren have identified five features central to personhood—consciousness, reasoning, self-motivated activity, the capacity to communicate, and self-awareness. Warren claims that a foetus is no more conscious or rational than a fish, and that accordingly abortion is not immoral. Opponents argue that these criteria are arbitrary, and point out that a young infant would also fail many of these tests thus legitimizing infanticide. Conservatives use 'slippery-slope' arguments against the liberal position, claiming that a secure line cannot be drawn at any one point in the development of the foetus. They suggest that such lines are vague and can usually be pushed back down the slope of foetal development towards conception as the only clear point of origin for individual human life.

A Buddhist pro-choice argument paralleling that based on the concept of personhood could be mounted by reference to the doctrine of the five 'aggregates' (*skandhas*). The five aggregates (shown in Box 12) are five defining characteristics of a human being. If it could be shown that these five characteristics were acquired gradually rather than all at once, it might be possible to establish a threshold before which the life of an early foetus was less valuable.

The second aggregate relating to the faculty of feeling, for instance, may be thought of as absent or not well developed in an embryo or very young foetus, since the capacity to feel depends on the development of a brain and central nervous system. The same might be said of the fifth aggregate, *vijñāna*, usually translated as 'consciousness', but which in this context means something more

Box 12 The five aggregates *(skandhas)*

1. material form (*rūpa*)
2. feelings and sensations (*vedanā*)
3. perceptions (*saṃjñā*)
4. volitions (*saṃskāra*)
5. consciousness (*vijñāna*)

like 'sentiency'. Such an argument faces the problem that according to the early commentarial tradition all five *skandhas* are present from the moment of rebirth (in other words, from conception). Buddhaghosa, for instance, states that the human mind–body aggregate (*nāma-rūpa*) is complete in the very first moment of existence as a human being. This means that the body (*rūpa*) and the other four aggregates of feelings (*vedanā*), conceptions (*saṃjñā*), mental formations (*saṃskāra*), and consciousness (*vijñāna*) form a unity from the outset rather than developing gradually as the foetus evolves.

The doctrine of rebirth, moreover, sees the new conceptus as not just a 'potential person' evolving for the first time from nothing, but as a continuing entity bearing the karmic encoding of a recently deceased individual. If we rewind the karmic tape a short way, perhaps just a few hours, to the point when death occurred in the previous life, we would typically find an adult man or woman fulfilling all the requirements of 'personhood'. The bodily form at rebirth has changed, but the bodily form of human beings changes constantly, and according to Buddhist teachings we have before us at conception the same individual only now once again at an immature stage of physical development. Given the continuity of the human subject through thousands of lifetimes, it seems arbitrary to apply labels such as 'actual' or 'potential' to any given stage and to claim that the individual repeatedly gains and loses the moral protection of the first precept.

It is sometimes suggested that Buddhism regards late abortions as morally worse than earlier ones. This view is based on a remark of Buddhaghosa in his commentary on the Vinaya (MA.i.198) to the effect that the size of the victim is one of two important criteria (the other being holiness) in assessing the gravity of breaches of the first precept. Since a foetus is considerably larger at the end of its term, it has been argued that late abortions are worse than earlier ones. This line of argument, however, fails to appreciate that Buddhaghosa's comments with respect to size were made purely with reference to animals. Thus, as we saw in Chapter 3, it is worse to kill a large animal, such as an elephant, than a fly, because it involves a greater degree of effort and determination, and the will to cause harm on the part of the assailant is greater. Clearly, the criterion of size is not meant to be applied in the case of human beings, otherwise it would lead to the ludicrous conclusion that killing large people was worse than killing small people. The argument that early abortions are morally less serious because the foetus is smaller, therefore, is based upon a misunderstanding of Buddhaghosa's criterion.

Abortion in Buddhist countries

In practice there is much deviation from the normative position we have seen described in the classical sources and a fair amount of 'moral dissonance' whereby individuals experience themselves as pulled in different directions. Table 1 gives an indication of the current legal position in selected Asian countries with large Buddhist populations, and in the next section we review in more detail the situation in two particular countries, Thailand and Japan, which follow the Theravāda and Mahāyāna forms of Buddhism respectively.

Thailand

In the more conservative Buddhist countries of south Asia abortion is illegal with certain limited exceptions. The *Thai Criminal Code* imposes strict penalties: a woman who causes an abortion for herself or procures one from someone else can expect to face a penalty of three years in prison or a fine, or both. The penalty for the abortionist is even greater: five years or a fine, or both, and if the woman is injured or killed in the process the penalties are more severe. Following a reform of the law in 1957 abortion is only permitted in cases of rape, incest, or sexual crimes, or when necessary to save the mother's life. Campaigns for further liberalization have so far been unsuccessful.

Table 1. Legality of abortion in selected Asian countries (2017)

Prohibited altogether	Laos
Permitted to save the life of the woman	Sri Lanka, Myanmar, Bhutan
…and preserve physical health	South Korea
…and preserve physical/mental health	Thailand
…and for socio-economic reasons	Japan, Taiwan
No restriction	Cambodia, Nepal, Vietnam

Source: Guttmacher Institute, Abortion in Asia, Fact Sheet, New York: Guttmacher Institute, 2018. Special conditions may apply in cases of rape, incest, and foetal abnormality.

Official statistics massively underestimate the number of abortions performed because illegal abortions are very common, with perhaps 300,000 such procedures a year performed in the many hundreds of illegal abortion clinics found throughout the country and particularly in rural areas. According to a 1987 study, the majority of abortions (around 80–90 per cent) were performed for married woman, mostly agricultural workers. The study also confirmed that abortion was the accepted method of birth control among these women, suggesting that if better contraception was available the number of abortions would drop sharply.

Despite the basic religious objection to abortion, Thai attitudes towards the issue are complex and researchers often encounter contradictory positions. A 1998 survey mainly of medical staff revealed ambivalent attitudes, with most respondents reporting negative feelings after the procedure, including 36 per cent who were concerned about the bad karma likely to result from it. While nearly all medical staff supported abortions for women who had been raped, who were HIV positive, or who had contracted German measles in the first trimester of pregnancy, 70 per cent were opposed to abortion on socio-economic grounds. Similarly, while a very high proportion of those surveyed viewed abortion as a threat to Thai values, 55 per cent of the medical staff favoured a liberalization of Thai abortion laws.

One interesting aspect of the Thai situation is the low profile maintained by Buddhist monks. With rare exceptions, monks do not picket abortion clinics, go on protest marches, or counsel women who are considering having an abortion, as clergy or support groups in the West might do. This is not because they have no position on the matter, and the *saṅgha* is widely perceived as belonging to the conservative wing of society that opposes abortion law reform. To a large extent this apparent aloofness has to do with matters of decorum and the high status in which the monkhood is held. As noted in our discussion of sexual ethics, most Buddhist layfolk, and particularly women, would feel embarrassment at discussing such intimate matters with monks, and prefer to discuss the problem with a doctor or other secular professional.

Japan

Elsewhere in Asia, attitudes and practices relating to abortion vary quite widely. In Japan (where Buddhism has been influential but is not the state religion), abortion is legal and some 300,000 abortions are performed each year. The issue of abortion has been particularly acute in Japan because the contraceptive pill was not widely available until 1999, largely because of concerns about side effects (some allege these were deliberately exaggerated by the medical profession). In the absence of effective prevention, an efficient (and profitable) abortion industry emerged to deal with the problem of unwanted pregnancies. Japanese society also evolved a strategy for coping with the anxiety such situations create in the form of the *mizuko kuyō* memorial service for aborted children. The ritual became extremely popular in the 1960s and 1970s when the number of abortions peaked at a million or more per annum according to some estimates.

6. Jizō Bosatsu.

Mizuko literally means 'water child', a concept that has its origins in Japanese mythology, and *kuyō* means a ritual or ceremony. The *mizuko kuyō* service is generally a simple one in which a small figure of the bodhisattva Jizō (see Figure 6) represents the departed child. Jizō Bosatsu is a popular bodhisattva in Japan. He is regarded as the protector of young children, and statues and shrines to him are found throughout the country. He is often shown dressed in the robes of a monk carrying a staff with six rings on it, which jingle like a child's rattle. The rings represent the six realms of rebirth in traditional Buddhist teachings, and Jizō visits each of these realms to help those in need.

Jizō's origins lie in India as the bodhisattva Kṣitigarbha, but when his cult reached Japan, he became associated with a folk-belief concerning the fate of children who die young, known as *mizuko* or 'water babies'. Such children were thought to go to an underworld or realm of the shades, a limbo where they awaited rebirth. In the popular imagination, this place was identified with a deserted river-bank called Sai-no-kawara which marks the boundary between this life and the next. There, the children seek to amuse themselves by day playing with pebbles on the beach, but when night comes they become cold and afraid, and it is then that Jizō comes to enfold them in his robe and cheer them with the jingling sound of his staff. This scene is often depicted in statues and described in hymns such as the one shown in Box 13 which is often recited in the course of the *mizuko kuyō* ritual.

Often a small image of Jizō (known as a *mizuko Jizō*) is decorated with a child's bib, and pinwheels and toys are placed alongside. Traditionally, the image would be placed in the home or at a small

Box 13 A hymn to Jizō often used in the *mizuko kuyō* liturgy

Be not afraid, little dear ones,
You were so little to come here,
All the long journey to Meido!
I will be Father and Mother,
Father and Mother and Playmate,
To all the children in Meido!
Then he caresses them kindly,
Folding his shining robes around them,
Lifting the smallest and frailest
Into his bosom, and holding
His staff for the stumblers to clutch.
To his long sleeves cling the infants,
Smile in response to his smiling,
Glad in his beauteous compassion.

roadside shrine, but in modern times specialist temples such as the Hasedera temple in Kamakura have appeared which offer commemorative services of various degrees of sophistication. These temples resemble memorial parks or cemeteries, with rows of small statues each commemorating a terminated pregnancy or miscarriage. The *mizuko kuyō* ceremony can take many forms, but would typically involve the parents, and sometimes other members of the family, erecting an image of Jizō (see Figure 7) and paying their respects by bowing, lighting a candle, striking gongs, chanting verses or a hymn, and perhaps reciting a short Buddhist *sūtra* such as the *Heart Sūtra*. It is also customary to provide a memorial tablet and a posthumous Buddhist name, which allows the deceased child to be recognized within the family structure. The rite may be repeated at intervals, such as on the anniversary of the abortion.

The public nature of the *mizuko kuyō* ceremonial simultaneously acknowledges the child that has been lost and helps those involved come to terms with the event on an emotional level (Box 14). Women who have the ritual performed find it consoling, and it is clearly comforting to think that Jizō is protecting their lost offspring. Many Western women who learn about *mizuko kuyō* feel the rite could be beneficial, and Jeff Wilson has explored how *mizuko kuyō* has been adapted for use in an American context.

The rite, however, is not without its critics. The majority of Buddhist organizations in Japan do not endorse *mizuko kuyō*, regarding it as a modern innovation based on questionable theology and lacking any basis in the *sūtras*. One of the largest Buddhist organizations in Japan, the Jōdō Shinshū, actively opposes the rite for this reason, pointing out that according to orthodox Buddhist teachings a ritual cannot wipe away the bad karma caused by an abortion. Some unscrupulous temples in Japan have also exploited the ritual commercially, promoting the idea of *tatari*, or retribution sought by departed spirits. The idea has been put about, often accompanied by lurid pictures, that an

7. Mizuko Jizō memorial at Raikoji (Kamakura, Japan).

Box 14 Verse from a popular song about the mizuko kuyō ceremony

The blessing of the child I had expected
Vanished like a dream.
How bitter not to be able to cuddle my child.
As I secretly visit the *mizuko* resting place
I offer this lotus flower from the last *kuyō*.
May it be a penitential proof of my love.

aborted foetus becomes a vengeful spirit that causes problems for the mother unless placated by the ritual. Undoubtedly, many temples saw the ritual simply as a money-making scheme and exploited vulnerable women.

Opposition on the part of the Jōdō Shinshū and others, however, has not taken a political form, and Japanese Buddhists have not campaigned to change the law on abortion or sought to influence the practice of the medical profession. Japan has not seen the picketing or attacks on abortion clinics that have taken place in the USA. Buddhism recognizes that the pressures and complexities of life can cloud the judgement and lead people to make wrong choices. The appropriate response in these cases, however, is thought to be compassion and understanding rather than condemnation.

Some Buddhists, especially in the West, feel that there is more to be said on the morality of abortion than is found in the ancient sources, and that there may be circumstances in which abortion is justified. For one thing, early Buddhist attitudes were formulated in a society that took a very different view of the status of women. Feminist writers have drawn attention to the patriarchal nature of traditional societies and to the institutionalized repression of women down the centuries (other scholars deny that either of these historical claims is correct, except at specific times and places). It has also been argued that abortion rights are integral to the emancipation of women and are necessary to redress injustice. Buddhists who are sympathetic to this view and who support the demand for 'reproductive rights' may recommend meditation and discussion with a Buddhist teacher as ways in which the woman can come to a decision in harmony with her conscience. As the encounter between Buddhism and Western values proceeds, discussions over the abortion question are certain to continue, hopefully producing more light and less heat than in the past.

Chapter 7
Suicide and euthanasia

On 11 June 1963, the 73-year-old Vietnamese monk Thich
Quang Duc burned himself alive on a main street in Saigon,
making headlines around the world. Sitting calmly in the lotus
posture, the elderly monk ordered two of his followers to douse
him with petrol and then calmly set himself alight (see Figure 8).
The American journalist David Halberstam witnessed the
dramatic scene:

> Flames were coming from a human being; his body was slowly
> withering and shriveling up, his head blackening and charring. In
> the air was the smell of burning flesh ... Behind me I could hear the
> sobbing of the Vietnamese who were now gathering. I was too
> shocked to cry, too confused to take notes or ask questions, too
> bewildered to even think.

In contrast to the shock and distress of those around him, the
venerable monk remained still and serene. The well-known
photograph reproduced here of him sitting calmly while his
body burned in the flames became one of the defining images of
the 1960s.

Thich Quang Duc's suicide was a protest against the religious
policies of the dictator Ngo Dinh Diem, who had persistently

8. Suicide of Buddhist monk Thich Quang Duc in Saigon, 1963.

favoured the country's Catholic minority. Thich Quang Duc's final testimony read:

> Before closing my eyes to go to Buddha, I have the honour to present
> my words to President Diem, asking him to be kind and tolerant
> towards his people and enforce a policy of religious equality.

Apart from the political statement it made, this dramatic image brought Buddhism to the attention of many in the West, and awakened curiosity about a religion whose followers could act with such conviction while manifesting a deep sense of inner peace and serenity and possessing apparently superhuman self-control.

What was the significance of this act, and how should it be assessed from an ethical perspective (Box 15)? Was Thich Quang Duc a martyr or a fanatic, and was his heroic self-sacrifice in

Box 15   Thich Nhat Hanh, *Vietnam: The Lotus in a Sea of Fire* (1967)

The press spoke then of suicide, but in the essence, it is not. It is not even a protest. What the monks said in the letters they left before burning themselves aimed only at alarming, at moving the hearts of the oppressors, and at calling the attention of the world to the suffering endured then by the Vietnamese. To burn oneself by fire is to prove that what one is saying is of the utmost importance... The Vietnamese monk, by burning himself, says with all his strength and determination that he can endure the greatest of sufferings to protect his people... To express will by burning oneself, therefore, is not to commit an act of destruction but to perform an act of construction, that is, to suffer and to die for the sake of one's people. This is not suicide.

accordance with Buddhist teachings? Buddhist leaders in Vietnam sanctioned his suicide, and that of another elderly monk, Thich Tieu Dieu, but apparently refused permission for younger monks to do likewise. The militant leader Thich Tri Quang declared, 'Burning oneself to death is the noblest form of struggle which symbolizes the spirit of nonviolence of Buddhism.' In the aftermath of this statement, five deaths occurred, at which point Tri Quang called on his followers to desist. In recent decades the policy of the Church has apparently been to dissuade its followers from killing themselves.

While some Buddhists interpreted these suicides as heroic acts of self-sacrifice in accordance with the bodhisattva ideal, others saw them as misguided and contrary to Buddhist teachings. For some they seemed to involve both violence and the squandering of a 'precious human rebirth'. The disagreements over the Vietnamese suicides illustrate the problematic nature of suicide as a moral issue. For one thing, we can never be completely sure of the motives of the person concerned, since he or she cannot be called to give evidence. Another complication is that it is not always easy to define what counts as 'suicide'. If we take as our definition of suicide something like 'cases where a person knowingly embarks on a course of action that will lead to her death', we may find the category too broad. For instance, is the soldier who throws himself on a grenade to save his comrades 'committing suicide'? And what of the martyr who refuses to recant knowing that the stake awaits him, or the pilot who remains at the controls of his aeroplane to avoid crashing into a school? Depending on how we classify these examples, our moral assessment can be very different. Rather than being associated with the stigma of suicide, these individuals may be praised and even regarded as heroes. The fact remains, however, that they all freely chose a course of action that they knew would end in their deaths.

Given the nuances that distinguish the different kinds of self-inflicted death, some commentators prefer to avoid pejorative terms like 'suicide' and speak instead of 'voluntary death'. Perhaps a separate category of 'altruistic suicide' is needed to encompass the examples cited above, and one of 'religious suicide' for cases like that of Thich Quang Duc. In discussions of both suicide and euthanasia, misunderstandings often arise due to a failure to provide definitions and clarify the issues at stake. I will say more about the term 'euthanasia' and its various nuances later in this chapter, but since the word 'suicide' is ingrained in our everyday language, I propose to retain it now that the reader has been alerted to the possible semantic pitfalls.

Self-immolation

When Thich Quang Duc dramatically ended his life in 1963, he set an example others would follow. In the decades since his death there have been several thousand deaths by burning all over the world, many directly modelled on his act. Most of the people who burn themselves as an act of public protest are young men, typically aged about 25. Following protests in 2008, a spate of self-immolations occurred among Tibetans, mainly in the Chinese provinces of Qinghai and Sichuan. Between 2009 and 2018, 155 Tibetans self-immolated, including 24 monks (or former monks) and 2 nuns. The Dalai Lama has refused to criticize their actions saying, 'If I criticize [them], then their family members may feel very sad.' Nevertheless, he believes their sacrifice has 'no effect and creates more problems'.

In China there are historical precedents for individuals burning themselves or parts of their bodies for religious reasons. Burning of the body in a token way has formed part of the monastic ordination ritual in China and Korea down to modern times. In the course of the ordination ceremony a small cone of incense is placed on the monk's shaven head and ignited. When it burns away, it leaves a permanent mark on the scalp. This practice, known as moxibustion, has ancient roots in China and was used in ceremonies designed to produce rain. Other, more dramatic, examples feature in the historical records, including burning fingers or entire limbs (usually the arms), and in extreme cases burning the whole body (Box 16). A 10th-century treatise by the Chinese monk Yongming Yanshou (904–75) commends these practices to ordinary monks and nuns (other authorities disagreed, arguing that such extreme acts were only appropriate for great bodhisattvas). Such deeds were seen by those who approved of them as sacrifices to the Buddha, recalling the master's own funeral cremation, and demonstrating great piety and devotion.

It is interesting, however, as James Benn has shown, that the two texts that validate these practices (the *Brahmajāla Sūtra* and the *Śūraṃgamasamādhi Sūtra*) are both apocryphal Chinese compositions that lack an Indian ancestor. The Buddhist pedigree of these fiery suicides is therefore open to question.

Suicide has also been common in neighbouring Japan in the ritualized form known as *seppuku* (or *hara kiri*) meaning 'to slice

Box 16   The *Brahmajāla Sūtra* (*Fan Wang Ching*)

A Chinese text from the 5th century CE explains how new bodhisattvas should be instructed by one who knows the scriptures and regulations of the Mahāyāna:

> In accordance with the Dharma he should explain to them all the ascetic practices, such as setting fire to the body, setting fire to the arm, or setting fire to the finger. If one does not set fire to the body, the arm or the finger as an offering to the Buddhas, one is not a renunciant bodhisattva. Moreover, one should sacrifice the feet, hands and flesh of the body as offerings to hungry tigers, wolves, and lions and to all hungry ghosts.

the abdomen'. This act involves making two small crosswise slices across the gut while in a kneeling position, after which an assistant would behead the subject with a sword (in practice the first step was rarely carried out). Beginning in the Tokugawa period, samurai warriors came to see this sacrifice as the penalty for a failure in their duty and as enjoined by their professional code of honour. In modern times, large numbers of suicides occurred among the Japanese military in the wake of the country's defeat in the Second World War. Since many samurai turned to Buddhism, some commentators have come to see suicide as legitimized by Buddhist teachings, and have gone so far as to claim that the practice of suicide was approved of by the Buddha. We need to examine these claims and consider to what extent the east Asian practices described so far have a foundation in the early teachings.

Suicide in Indian Buddhism

The notion that suicide is permitted in early Buddhism has gained currency largely because of a small number of cases reported in the Pali canon where monks who were sick and in pain took their own lives and apparently received a posthumous endorsement from the Buddha. A special feature of these cases is that the monks in question attained *arhatship* as they died and so were not reborn. Based on these examples, something of a consensus has emerged that while Buddhism is generally opposed to suicide it makes an exception in the case of the enlightened, since they in some sense have transcended conventional moral norms. My own reading of the sources is more cautious, and suggests that while the Buddha clearly felt great sympathy for those involved he did not actively condone suicide. His general position seems to have been that suicide is wrong, but that we should not judge too harshly those who take their lives *in extremis*.

Apart from these special cases, there is little support for suicide elsewhere in the early sources, and in general it is strongly discouraged. We see this in the reaction of the *arhat* Śāriputra when he learns in one of the cases mentioned above that the monk Channa is contemplating 'using the knife' to end his suffering:

> Let the venerable Channa not use the knife! Let the venerable Channa live—we want the venerable Channa to live! If he lacks suitable food, I will go in search of suitable food for him. If he lacks suitable medicine, I will go in search of suitable medicine for him. If he lacks a proper attendant, I will attend on him. Let the venerable Channa not use the knife! Let the venerable Channa live—we want the venerable Channa to live! (M.iii.264)

These comments reflect the broad position of the early tradition, namely that acts of violence should be avoided and death—including one's own—should never be caused intentionally.

One of the few places where suicide is discussed in detail is in the Vinaya under the rubric of the third *pārājika*, the rule prohibiting the taking of human life. This rule has already been mentioned several times, including in the discussion of abortion in Chapter 6. The circumstances in which the rule was introduced have a direct bearing on suicide and euthanasia. The commentary to the third *pārājika* relates how on one occasion the Buddha gave instruction to the monks on a specific form of meditation known as 'contemplation of the impure'. This is a method used to counteract attachment. In practising it, one reflects upon the body as impermanent, a thing subject to decay and corruption, and not a proper object of attachment.

Having instructed the monks on this theme, the Buddha retired into seclusion for a fortnight. Unfortunately, the monks became overzealous in their practice and developed disgust and loathing for their bodies. So intense did this feeling become that many felt death would be preferable to such a repulsive existence. Accordingly, they proceeded to kill themselves, and lent assistance to one another in doing so. They found an assistant who agreed to assist by killing the monks in return for their robes and bowls. When the Buddha learned what had taken place, he proclaimed the third *pārājika* (Box 17). This episode shows the Buddha directly intervening to prevent monks committing suicide either by their own hand or with the assistance of others, and gives grounds for thinking that this reflects the normative Buddhist position.

Box 17 The third *pārājika*, the monastic rule prohibiting taking human life

Should any monk intentionally deprive a human being of life or look about so as to be his knife-bringer, or eulogise death, or incite [anyone] to death saying 'My good man, what need have you of this evil, difficult life? Death would be better for you than life'—or who should deliberately and purposefully in various ways eulogise death or incite anyone to death: he is also one who is defeated, he is not in communion.

(Vin.iii.72)

It will be noted that the rule the Buddha introduced prohibits assisting others to commit suicide, not suicide itself. The reason for this is likely to be the technical one that the monastic rules are drawn up with a view to imposing sanctions and penalties on those who break them. In the case of a person who has killed himself, this question clearly does not arise.

It appears that the dramatic cases of suicide by auto-cremation we have discussed have no antecedents in the early tradition, and that the east Asian practices of self-immolation and *seppuku* originated outside Buddhism and have their roots in the indigenous local cultures. While these facts do not by themselves mean that suicide is immoral, they make it more difficult to claim that it was approved of by the Buddha. The general tenor of the early teachings, with their strong emphasis on non-violence, seems at odds with the kind of self-mutilation and destruction of the human body practised in parts of east Asia.

Euthanasia

The discussion of assisted suicide in the third *pārājika* leads naturally to the issue of euthanasia. By 'euthanasia' here is meant intentionally causing death by act or omission in the context of medical care. We will confine our discussion to *voluntary* euthanasia, that is, when a mentally competent patient freely requests medical help in ending her life. Two principal modes of euthanasia are commonly distinguished, namely active and passive.

Active euthanasia is the deliberate killing of a patient by an act, for example by lethal injection. Passive euthanasia is the intentional causing of death by omission, for example by failing to provide food, medicine, or some other requisite for life. Some commentators see this distinction as morally significant, whereas others do not. Given the importance Buddhism places on intention, it would seem to matter little whether the fatal outcome is achieved by active or passive means. Note that on the definition in use here the borderline case of administering painkillers which may simultaneously hasten death does not count as euthanasia of either kind, since the doctor's intention in such circumstances is to kill the pain, not the patient.

There is no term synonymous with 'euthanasia' in early Buddhist sources, nor is the morality of the practice discussed in a systematic way. Given that monks were active as medical practitioners, however, circumstances occasionally arose when the value of life was called into question. These circumstances are outlined in a number of the case histories preserved in the Vinaya. In the sixty or so cases reported, about one-third are concerned with deaths that occurred following medical intervention by monks. In some of these cases, the death of a patient was thought desirable for 'quality of life' reasons such as the avoidance of protracted terminal care (Vin.ii.79) or to minimize the suffering of patients with serious disabilities.

The context in which the third *pārājika* arose is particularly important in relation to euthanasia since the case for allowing euthanasia rests on the postulate that 'death would be better than life', especially when, to use the wording of the precept, life seems 'evil and difficult'. As noted, the precept is directed specifically at those who lend assistance to others in ending their lives, which the precept calls 'acting as knife-bringer'. This would seem to apply to all forms of euthanasia, and also physician-assisted suicide, in which the physician assists the person who wishes to die by prescribing—but not administering—lethal drugs.

As noted in Chapter 1, compassion is an important Buddhist moral value, and some sources reveal an increasing awareness of how a commitment to the alleviation of suffering can create a conflict with the principle of non-harming (*ahiṃsā*). Compassion, for example, might lead one to take life in order to alleviate suffering, and indeed is one of the main grounds on which euthanasia is commonly advocated. The issue of euthanasia performed for compassionate reasons (often called 'mercy killing') comes up in the Vinaya in the first of the cases to be reported after the precept against killing was declared (Vin.ii.79). In this case, the motive for bringing about the death of the patient is said to have been compassion (*karuṇā*) for the suffering of a dying monk.

According to the commentator Buddhaghosa, those found guilty in this case took no direct action to terminate life but merely suggested to a dying monk that death would be preferable to his present condition. Despite this apparently benevolent motive, namely to spare a dying person unnecessary pain, the judgement of the Buddha was that those involved were guilty of a breach of the precept. What had they done wrong? In Buddhaghosa's analysis the essence of their wrongdoing was that the guilty monks 'made death their aim' (*maraṇa-atthika*) (VA.ii.464). It would therefore appear immoral from a Buddhist perspective to embark on a course of action whose aim is the destruction of human life, regardless of the quality of the agent's motive. From this we may conclude that while compassion is always a morally good motive, it does not justify whatever is done in its name.

Another moral principle often invoked in the debate on euthanasia is autonomy. This involves the claim that the free choices of rational individuals should be respected, including the right to dispose of one's life as one sees fit. Buddhism would endorse this principle up to a point, since the doctrine of karma teaches that individuals have free will and are responsible for their moral choices. However, it also seems to want to place some limit on the scope of this freedom, as can be seen from the circumstances of the third *pārājika*. The monks involved here were, as far as we can tell, competent, rational adults. They wished to die because they had made the judgement that their lives were not worth living and that they would be better off dead. This was a free choice following an evaluation of their quality of life, which they deemed to be insufficient to justify continued existence. In terms of respect for autonomy, therefore, their decision might be thought justifiable, in the sense that as competent adults it was up to them to dispose of their lives as they saw fit. It seems, however, that the Buddha did not agree.

There appears to be no strong demand for the legalization of euthanasia by Buddhists today. Few, if any, Buddhist groups have campaigned for it, and euthanasia has not been made legal in any Buddhist country. Rather than seek to introduce euthanasia as an option in terminal care, it seems many Buddhists would support the ideals of the hospice movement. In the West, the San Francisco Zen Center has offered facilities for the dying since 1971 and started a full-scale training programme for hospice workers in 1987. In 1986, the Buddhist Hospice Trust was founded in the UK. This organization exists to explore Buddhist thinking on matters relating to death, dying, and bereavement and provides access to a network of volunteers who visit the dying and bereaved at their request.

Must life be preserved at all costs?

Does the Buddhist opposition to euthanasia mean that life must be preserved at all costs? At one point in his commentary, Buddhaghosa has a brief but interesting discussion about the situation of terminally ill patients in which two contrasting scenarios are mentioned.

If one who is sick ceases to take food with the intention of dying when medicine and nursing care are at hand, he commits a minor offence (*dukkata*). But in the case of a patient who has suffered a long time with a serious illness the nursing monks may become weary and turn away in despair thinking 'when will we ever cure him of this illness?' Here it is legitimate to decline food and medical care if the patient sees that the monks are worn out and his life cannot be prolonged even with intensive care. (VA.ii.467)

The contrast here is between the patient who rejects medical care with the express purpose of ending his life, and one who resigns himself to the inevitability of death after medical resources have been exhausted. The moral distinction is that the first patient seeks death or 'makes death his aim', while the second simply accepts the proximity and inevitability of death and rejects further treatment or nourishment as pointless. Thus, while the first patient wishes to die, the second does not seek death but is resigned to the fact that he is beyond medical help.

The scenario described by Buddhaghosa suggests that Buddhism does not believe there is a moral obligation to preserve life at all costs. Recognizing the inevitability of death is, of course, a central element in Buddhist teachings. Death cannot be postponed forever, and Buddhists are encouraged to be mindful and prepared for the evil hour when it comes. To seek to prolong life beyond its natural span by recourse to ever-more elaborate medical interventions when no cure or recovery is in sight is a denial of human mortality and would be seen as arising from craving (*tṛṣṇā*) and delusion (*moha*).

Following the above line of reasoning, in terminal care situations, including those in which patients have been conclusively diagnosed as being in a 'persistent vegetative state' (PVS), there would be no need to go to disproportionate lengths to provide treatment when there is little or no prospect of recovery. For example, there would be no requirement to treat complications like pneumonia by administering antibiotics. While it might be foreseen that an untreated infection would lead to the patient's death, it would also be recognized that any course of treatment must be assessed in the light of the overall prognosis. Rather than embarking on a series of piecemeal treatments, none of which would produce a net improvement in the patient's overall condition, it would often be appropriate to reach the conclusion that the patient was beyond medical help and let events take their course.

Many Buddhists believe that lifespan is determined by karma, and that death will come at the appointed time. To shorten life artificially through suicide or euthanasia is seen as interfering with one's karmic destiny. Before passing judgement, however, we would be wise to enquire as to the motivation and circumstances of each case. There is a world of difference between the tragic suicide of a depressed teenager and the altruistic self-immolation of a Thich Quang Duc. Today, the morality of euthanasia and physician-assisted suicide are hotly debated topics, and no doubt Buddhists in different jurisdictions will find themselves on opposite sides of the debate, just as Chinese Buddhists in the 10th century disagreed on whether it was right to burn limbs.

Buddhism has a great openness about death and encourages its followers to meditate on death and prepare for it in practical ways. The death of the Buddha is the example most Buddhists would seek to emulate. Despite being 80 years old and having suffered painful illnesses in the last months of his life, he faced death serenely. We are told that a few months before his death he 'mindfully rejected the life-principle' (D.ii.107). While some take this to mean that he 'committed suicide', it most likely means he accepted that the end was near and resolved not to make further efforts to prolong his life. As always, he thought more of others than himself: only after giving his disciples a final opportunity to ask questions and clear up any remaining doubts about his teachings did he enter final nirvana.

Chapter 8
Clones, cyborgs, and singularities

Buddhism has so far largely steered clear of damaging confrontations with science, but new technologies call into question basic Buddhist teachings like karma and rebirth. Innovative methods for the enhancement of mind and body, furthermore, promise a technological shortcut to nirvana and eternal life without the need for lifetimes of practice. Some even foresee a time when human beings will exist in a purely digital form, thus solving once and for all the problems of old age, sickness, and death that give Buddhism its *raison d'être*. Here we ask first to what extent new technologies like cloning, gene editing, and cryogenics challenge traditional beliefs in karma and rebirth before considering whether Buddhism shares the optimistic Transhumanist vision of the future course of human evolution.

Cloning and genetics

The birth of Dolly the sheep caused a furore when it was announced to the world on 24 February 1997. What made this birthday so special was that Dolly had been produced by means of a new technology that threatens to revolutionize the way we think about the basis of life. A clone is a genetic duplicate—a kind of photocopy—of another individual. In conventional reproduction, each parent contributes 23 of the 46 chromosomes that will determine the child's genetic identity. A cloned child, however, inherits all 46 of its chromosomes from a single DNA source.

In the furore that followed the birth of Dolly, cloning met with widespread condemnation. Religious opposition was led by the theistic traditions. These religions teach that life is a gift from God, and for them the creation of life in the laboratory seems to usurp the divine authority of the creator. Reproductive cloning is also in conflict with the biblical model of sexual generation, and in the eyes of many believers threatens to undermine divinely sanctioned norms governing family and social life.

Many of these theological objections disappear when cloning is viewed from a Buddhist perspective. Since Buddhism does not believe in a supreme being, there is no divine creator who might be offended by human attempts to duplicate his work. Nor does Buddhism believe in a personal soul or teach that human beings are made in God's image. Its view of creation and cosmology is very different from that of the Bible and does not entail normative principles about human reproduction of the kind discussed in Chapter 4. There is no theological reason, then, why cloning could not be seen as another way of creating life, neither intrinsically better nor worse than any other. Such is the opinion of Professor Yong Moon, a member of a cloning team at Seoul National University who stated, 'Cloning is a different way of thinking about the recycling of life—it's a Buddhist way of thinking.' Be that as it may, cloning presents certain conundrums for Buddhist doctrine.

One of the first books to make a positive case for human cloning was *Who's Afraid of Human Cloning* by Gregory E. Pence. Pence began his book with the following statement.

> Buddhist scholar Donald Lopez foresees real problems for the
> theory of karma. Would the clone inherit the karma of the original
> person? And he wonders 'What did the sheep do in a previous life
> that resulted in its being cloned in this one?'

The answer to the first question is relatively straightforward and can be found by considering the case of identical (or 'monozygotic') twins. Like a clone (which is in effect what they are) these twins have identical DNA, but there is no reason to think they share identical karma. In fact, Buddhaghosa informs us that twins differ in subtle physical ways as well as in their mannerisms and so forth and explains this as due precisely to their different karma. If identical twins do not share the same karma there seems no reason to suppose that a clone will share the karma of its DNA donor. It seems axiomatic in Buddhist teachings that no two individuals can share the same karma (in effect, this would mean they were the same person).

As regards the second question, as to what the sheep did in a previous life to result in its being cloned in this one, two points can be made. The first is that the question arises from a misunderstanding of karma. As mentioned in Chapter 1, karma is not deterministic, so there is no reason to assume that being cloned has a karmic cause. The second is that Buddhism regards speculation about past causes as unprofitable: even assuming there is some karmic cause, what matters is not what we did in the past but what we do now.

Apart from problems with karma and rebirth, cloning raises other puzzling questions, such as whether it is possible to clone a Buddha. Assuming that the Buddha had human DNA, there seems no reason why he could not be cloned, perhaps using DNA from a relic. The result would be a genetic duplicate similar to the kind seen in the case of identical twins. The interesting question, however, is whether the resemblance would be purely a physical one or whether the clone would also be an enlightened being. The answer to this question depends on the view we take of the role of DNA in bringing about the state of enlightenment.

Buddhas are thought to have a deep insight into the nature of things, and it seems unlikely such a state of consciousness could be encoded in the structure of DNA. This makes it difficult to see how there could be anything like a 'Buddha gene' which serves as the genetic marker for enlightenment. We are told that the Buddha's enlightenment was the result of lifetimes of spiritual practice, which the possession of a 'Buddha gene' would have rendered unnecessary. It also follows that if enlightenment depended on a genetic trait, those who lacked the appropriate DNA would be excluded from the goal of Buddhahood, but there is nothing in mainstream Buddhism, at least, to suggest that anyone is congenitally excluded from this goal.

A further problem is that karma and genetics provide competing explanations for certain physical and mental characteristics. The Buddha explained differences in lifespan (*āyus*), illness (*ābādha*), physical appearance (*varṇa*), and intellectual ability (*prajñā*) as being due to karma (M.iii.202f.). However, genetics now informs us that these characteristics are to a considerable extent influenced by genes. It also tells us that the individual human genome is entirely determined by parental DNA, and since the parents pre-exist the child it seems impossible for the karma of an as-yet unconceived child to modify the DNA it will inherit from its parents. So, if the characteristics the Buddha attributed to karma are in fact determined by DNA, is the concept of karma redundant?

Early assumptions that DNA is strongly deterministic, however, appear to be incorrect, and the emerging field of epigenetics suggests that there is considerable indeterminacy in the way genes are expressed. This is one reason the rapid medical progress expected following the sequencing of the human genome in 2000 has not so far occurred. It seems that no single gene is strongly predictive, and genetic switches called 'enhancers' play a role in activating and deactivating genes in a way that is so far not well understood.

Factors like environment and behaviour can also influence the way genes are activated, if they are activated at all. Thus, while members of the same family may have a genetic disposition for diabetes or asthma, only one may develop the condition due to lifestyle factors (e.g. by smoking or consuming excess sugar). Similarly, a person may be born with a genetic disposition for intelligence, but if this capacity is not nurtured by a sound moral education, it is unlikely to bear fruit as wisdom.

Since past karma is held to influence choices made in the present lifetime, including choices about such things as diet and lifestyle, we can see how karma could play a role in shaping mental and physical development. At the same time, karma does not exclude the role of accidents. The fate of a given individual is then perhaps best understood as not determined exclusively by DNA but by a combination of genetic disposition, lifestyle choices, environment, and random events, all interacting in complex ways.

However, the problem we have raised extends beyond genetics. The sources state that karma determines things such as the socio-economic status of the family into which a child is born. As we saw in Chapter 6, this was traditionally explained by the notion of the consciousness of a deceased person (*gandharva*) being drawn to rebirth in a particular womb. Where fertilization occurs outside the bedroom, however, as with in-vitro fertilization (IVF), such an explanation sounds implausible. Some more convincing explanation of the mechanism of rebirth seems required.

Given such conundrums, some Western Buddhists prefer to remain agnostic about karma. Others, known as 'Buddhist modernists', reject belief in karma and rebirth entirely, dismissing these notions as 'cultural baggage' that can now be jettisoned. The traditional cosmological beliefs, however, are woven into the fabric of Buddhist teachings and are not easily disentangled. The Buddha said that on the night of his enlightenment he recalled many of his past lives, and if we reject this testimony as false it is hard to know what criterion we can use to determine the veracity of his other statements.

Gene editing

Another area in which genetics raises ethical dilemmas is in the field of gene editing. The aim of this technique is to remedy genetic abnormalities and alleviate hereditary diseases. Treatments of this kind, which are known as 'somatic' therapies, work by repairing genetically abnormal cells. In 2012 scientists developed a new tool to modify genes that has revolutionized the field of molecular biology. This goes by the acronym CRISPR ('clustered regularly interspaced short palindromic repeats') and is often described as a pair of 'molecular scissors' that allows scientists to cut and paste genes at will in animals, plants, and human beings. The technique is relatively simple and has many potential uses. There are hopes it can be used to delete genes that prevent the immune system from attacking cancer cells, correct defective genes responsible for diseases like sickle cell anaemia and Duchenne muscular dystrophy, produce new antibiotics, eliminate mosquito-borne diseases, and eliminate viruses in crops.

The consequences of tinkering with genes in these ways are not yet fully understood and possible side effects include 'off-target' mutations leading to pathologies like cancer. Because of these risks, leading scientists agreed a moratorium in 2015 on the use of CRISPR to modify gametes (sperm or eggs) or embryo cells—a technique known as 'germ line' editing. This was to avoid the risk of a modified human genome being passed on to future generations and potentially altering the human gene pool with unforeseeable consequences. In 2018, however, Chinese scientist He Jiankui broke the moratorium and announced the birth of the world's first CRISPR babies, twin girls nicknamed Lulu and Nana.

Dr He altered the genes of the embryos in an attempt to make their cells resistant to the HIV virus. Despite the widespread condemnation of these experiments, Dr He stated, 'we believe ethics are on our side of history'. Supporters of such research point out that although the risks of germ-line therapy are great, so too are the potential benefits, and believe that the prospect of freeing future offspring from the misery of an inherited disease tips the balance in favour of experimentation.

What can be said about the ethics of gene editing from a Buddhist perspective? There seems to be no great problem when the CRISPR technique is used to cure a genetic abnormality in an individual patient who consents to the treatment. When used in germ-line therapy, however, Buddhists would have similar reservations to those noted above in connection with alterations to heritable DNA. There is also concern about the creation of 'designer babies', or babies who are produced to a specification supplied by their parents with respect to traits like intelligence and athleticism. Various reservations have been expressed in this regard, from the erosion of human dignity (the baby is seen as simply a product of technology) to a return to the eugenics programmes of the 1930s and 1940s. Unequal access to the technology could also increase social inequality and result in humans becoming divided into subspecies. Scientist Stephen Hawking's last prediction was that the wealthiest in society would soon begin to edit the DNA of their offspring to produce a superhuman race thereby dividing humanity into genetic 'haves' and 'have nots'.

Quite apart from the risks surrounding the technique itself, any such experimentation must also be subject to the same moral standards that apply to any other activity. From a Buddhist perspective, this means that the motivation of those involved must be wholesome (free from greed, hatred, and delusion) and the reasonably foreseeable consequences for individuals and society at large must be taken into account. As we have seen, not all scientific research meets these standards, and the scandal surrounding Dr He is reminiscent of an earlier one involving Korean scientist Hwang Woo-Suk who falsely claimed in 2004 that he had succeeded in cloning human embryos.

Cryonics

Genetic research offers one way of curing disease and increasing longevity, but there are many more. The Alcor Life Extension Foundation of Arizona defines cryonics as 'the science of using ultra-cold temperature to preserve human life with the intent of restoring good health when technology becomes available to do so'. Cryopreservation is an experimental technique which aims at freezing and later resuscitating people who have died. Either the head or the whole body can be frozen. Today, embryos are routinely frozen and resuscitated, suggesting that life can be sustained in suspended animation over long periods of time, although it has not so far proved possible to cryopreserve human organs for transplantation.

In the case of the brain, some researchers believe that cryonics need not resuscitate the organ itself, but simply preserve the information it contains for later download. In terms of this theory, personality, memory, and skills are encoded in the pattern or connection between neurons rather than physically embedded in the organ. In 2018 scientists working at cryobiology company 21st Century Medicine successfully froze and rewarmed a complete pig's brain with its connectome (the wiring diagram of the brain's neural connections) still intact. This meant that the information stored in the brain's 150 trillion connections could—if the theory is sound—be recovered and uploaded into a new physical or virtual body.

Even assuming cryonics is shown to be successful, however, there are social aspects to be considered. It is not clear, for example, how someone would fare in the far-distant future without friends or family, and the kind of welcome received might not be the cordial one expected. Nevertheless, there are people willing to take the risk. There are currently almost 300 cryonically frozen individuals in the USA, some fifty in Russia, and several thousand more signed up for the procedure, including Google's Director of Engineering, Ray Kurzweil.

Once again, we might wonder whether this new technology undermines the Buddhist belief in rebirth. Buddhism teaches that rebirth occurs soon after death (either instantaneously or at the latest forty days after death), and if a person's consciousness had already left the body, it would seem impossible for the resuscitation of a frozen brain or body to take place because the departed person would presumably by then have been reborn elsewhere.

Much, of course, turns on what one understands by 'death', and perhaps someone declared dead on today's criteria might be easily resuscitated in the future. If such a patient were to be cryogenically preserved before any deterioration in the brain had occurred (the patient could opt for euthanasia, where legal, to improve the chance of success), there would seem to be a reasonable prospect of resuscitation at a future date. If a cryogenically frozen patient was successfully restored to life centuries later, we might say that from a Buddhist perspective the patient never really passed away. What happened was that he or she was placed on long-term life-support, and since no one died, no one was reborn. The patient who was resuscitated, then, was the same as the one who 'died'.

Speculating further, we might ask whether the consciousness of a deceased person could take rebirth in an artificial body. Perhaps all bodies, whether carbon or silicon based, are best thought of simply as platforms for rebirth. Up to now, the latter have not been available, but developments in cybernetics might change that. Some Tibetan lamas, including the Dalai Lama, seem to think that a spiritually advanced person might consciously choose to take rebirth in a silicon-based body instead of a carbon-based human one.

Transhumanism

It is clear that genetics, neuroscience, artificial intelligence (Figure 9), and other new technologies are revolutionizing the way we think about ourselves. 'Transhumanists' see human beings as on the cusp of an evolutionary quantum leap that will overcome many of their present limitations: bodies will be enhanced with bionic limbs, and brains boosted by cybernetic implants and nanobots that increase intelligence and cognitive skills. One author defines Transhumanism as follows:

> Transhumanism is a class of philosophies of life that seek the continuation and acceleration of the evolution of intelligent life beyond its currently human form and human limitations by means of science and technology, guided by life-promoting principles and values. (Max More, 1990)

9. A robot modelled after the bodhisattva Kannon (Avalokiteśvara) gives its first teachings at the Kodaiji temple in Kyoto on 23 February 2019.

To many, biological immortality seems a realistic and desirable goal. Some Transhumanists envisage a merger between the fields of artificial intelligence (AI) and robotics, culminating in the 'Singularity'(see Figure 10), or the point at which human and machine consciousness merge to bring into being a new hybrid form of life, sometimes known as a 'cyborg'. These super-intelligent and long-lived beings, it is believed, will enjoy happiness and fulfilment impossible for ordinary mortals. Beyond this lies the ultimate goal of an altogether new mode of existence as a disembodied 'digital person' residing in a virtual reality hosted by a (hopefully benevolent) AI.

To encourage the development of AI along ethical lines a team of concerned experts and entrepreneurs launched OpenAI in

10. **Ray Kurzweil believes the Singularity is close at hand.**

2015. With a billion dollars of initial funding the organization hopes to promote dialogue among stakeholders and avoid the accidental creation of a malicious superintelligence that could ultimately destroy the human race. The associated challenge of teaching a machine to act ethically while avoiding the inevitable human prejudice and bias of its programmers is a task that will clearly require careful thought.

A Transhumanist manifesto called the Transhumanist Declaration was drafted in 1998 by twenty-three Transhumanist thinkers, and serves as the platform for Humanity Plus, an organization that promotes Transhumanist ideals. The declaration speaks in article one of 'the possibility of broadening human potential by overcoming aging, cognitive shortcomings, involuntary suffering, and our confinement to planet Earth'. The means to achieve this include 'techniques...to assist memory, concentration, and mental energy; life extension therapies; reproductive choice technologies; cryonics procedures; and many other possible human modification and enhancement technologies' (article eight).

Several articles of the Declaration make reference to ethical values. Article seven, for instance, states, 'Policy making ought to be guided by responsible and inclusive moral vision, taking seriously both opportunities and risks, respecting autonomy and individual rights, and showing solidarity with and concern for the interests and dignity of all people around the globe.' It adds, 'We must also consider our moral responsibilities towards generations that will exist in the future.' In the same vein, article eight affirms, 'We advocate the well-being of all sentience, including humans, non-human animals, and any future artificial intellects, modified life forms, or other intelligences to which technological and scientific advance may give rise.' We shall say more about these aims later.

Neurodharma

As seen in the Declaration just mentioned, the goal of Transhumanism is the noble one of overcoming pain, suffering, sickness, and death, the very obstacles to happiness that are mentioned in the First Noble Truth of Buddhism. For this reason, some see the aims of Buddhism and Transhumanism as convergent.

Buddhist meditators have for some time been working with neuroscientists in a partnership of 'lama and lab' to understand the phenomenon of neuroplasticity—the brain's capacity to change itself. The Dalai Lama proudly describes himself as 'half Buddhist monk, half scientist'. With the assistance of advanced practitioners, Western scientists have made significant progress toward understanding how meditative techniques work. Based on these discoveries, some now suggest that traditional meditative practices can be integrated with emerging neurotechnologies in order to enhance self-control, compassion, and insight.

A number of apps and devices are being developed to help the practitioner 'hack the brain' and experience the benefits of meditation without spending painful hours in the lotus posture. At present these devices are crude, but with further development it may be possible to induce higher states of trance (*dhyāna*) or flashes of insight (*satori*). And further down the line why not enlightenment itself?

Buddhist Transhumanists like James J. Hughes and Michael La Torra believe that emerging technologies can help build an environment that maximizes capacity for spiritual growth. Hughes is co-founder of the Institute for Ethics and Emerging Technologies and a participant in the Institute's 'Cyborg Buddha' project. He believes spiritual growth can be enhanced through neurotechnology, the use of stimulants, designer 'smart' drugs, and other psychoactive substances that enhance intelligence: just as psychiatric medications can help people with depression lead a normal life, so tweaking brain chemistry, it is suggested, could heighten the perception of ordinary people providing a techno-boost that allowed them to see the world in a more enlightened way. While the effect of such enhancement may not be permanent, it could be potentially life-changing.

We discussed the importance of moral virtues in Buddhist ethics in Chapter 2, and Hughes believes that moral enhancement by means of 'virtue engineering' may be possible through technological means. For example, if compassion is influenced by inherited genetic disposition, and activated through neurochemistry, it might be possible through a combination of genetic engineering and neurotechnology to strengthen the tendency to experience and exhibit compassion consistently.

While most of the discussion around moral enhancement has focused so far on boosting empathy, Hughes argues, not unreasonably, that a mature moral character requires the combining of multiple virtues such as self-control, compassion, and wisdom. He believes certain of these virtues can be enhanced with electronic, pharmaceutical, and genetic technologies. Conscientiousness and self-discipline, for example, seem to be linked to the dopamine receptor; the hormone oxytocin induces feelings of trust and bonding; and anger and aggression appear to be affected by the monoamine oxidase A gene (MAOA). Sceptics, however, point out that sound moral judgement depends on a balance of emotional, motivational, and cognitive factors, and that the bio-enhancement of only one of these may lead to a distorted moral conscience.

Concerns

Some Buddhists are uneasy about artificial enhancement and point out that the fifth precept prohibits the use of intoxicants.

Buddhism does not, however, prohibit the use of medicine, and a relevant distinction seems to be whether one consumes substances to get well or to get 'high'. Provided the aim is not simply to experience pleasure the fifth precept seems to present no obstacle to the use of non-addictive substances that enhance self-awareness. What the precept objects to, after all, is the taking of substances that 'lead to a loss of mindfulness (*apramāda*)'. Anything that *increases* mindfulness would then appear to be in accordance with the spirit of the precept.

At the same time, a distinction can be drawn between 'treatment' and 'enhancement', and the task of medicine is normally thought of as curing defects rather than making improvements. The line between the two, however, is blurred, and the titanium orthopaedic implants in use today, for example, seem to be both a treatment and an enhancement insofar as they are more durable than the joints that nature provides. As technology advances, moreover, what today is seen as enhancement may tomorrow be seen as routine treatment.

Apart from moral improvement, a central Transhumanist aim is the extension of lifespan. Calico—The California Life Company—was set up by the founders of Google in 2013 to find ways to combat ageing and its effects, and the annual RAAD conference ('Revolution Against Aging and Death') showcases the latest techniques for life extension. These include age-suppressing pro-biotics, parabiosis (infusing the body with younger blood cells), and drugs and other agents to protect telomeres (the part of a cell that affects ageing).

There seems no fundamental Buddhist objection to living longer, and the prolongation of life is a basic aim of Buddhist medicine. One obvious benefit of a longer life is that those committed to following the bodhisattva path can do more good than if their lives were cut short. Buddhist mythology, moreover, envisages the human lifespan as elastic, as lengthening or shortening in step with cosmic cycles. The lifespan of the gods is many times greater than that of human beings, although a vastly extended lifespan is not necessarily a greater good from a soteriological perspective. This is because life as a human being provides a 'reality check' in bringing one face to face with the painful realities of birth, old age, sickness, and death and it may be that it is the very experience of impermanence that makes enlightenment possible. Death, perhaps, is the grit in the oyster that produces the pearl of wisdom and gives life its meaning. As the philosopher Bertrand Russell expressed it, 'If I lived forever the joys of life would inevitably in the end lose their savor. As it is, they remain perennially fresh.'

Another common objection to Transhumanist immortality is that the desire to live forever is misguided because it assumes the existence of a self, which Buddhism denies. Transhumanists have a reply, however, which is that rather than seeking to preserve an unchanging self, what extending one's lifetime can do—especially if this involves uploading one's personality and memory to a cyber-host or merging with a higher intelligence—is enable a greater connection to others. By becoming part of a vast network, the sense of self would be diminished. Indeed, it may be that physical embodiment is a significant obstacle to perceiving the truth of no-self. Furthermore, if awakened beings form part of the same network, the prospects for achieving enlightenment may be greatly enhanced. What could be more helpful than a 24/7 connection to the mind of an enlightened teacher?

The Transhumanist message is certainly seductive: who would not want to live in a world without death or suffering? However, some see a tension in the Transhumanist Declaration between the utilitarian imperative to seek 'the well-being of all sentience', while at the same time 'respecting autonomy and individual rights'.

Critics allege that individual rights and freedoms will inevitably be sidelined in the dash by large corporations led by visionary entrepreneurs to implement new technologies which will be limited to the rich.

Political scientists Jürgen Habermas and Francis Fukuyama have expressed concern that Transhumanism as a political ideology will undermine the values of the liberal state and lead to a dystopic society. Fukuyama asks what will become of society if human nature is reconfigured such that citizens become more docile and manageable as envisaged in Aldous Huxley's *Brave New World* (1932). He warns that Transhumanity's social engineering may be a back door to dehumanization and the return of totalitarianism. Advocates like Hughes, however, believe that the utilitarian goals of Transhumanism can be balanced by the development of personal virtues.

Some see in the penumbra of the Transhumanist Declaration an ideology that makes scientific reasoning the ultimate authority and denigrates belief-systems based on religious or spiritual truth. These sceptics reject the Transhumanist claim that the best way to fix human problems is through science and technology. They point out that there have been technological developments throughout human history, from the invention of the wheel onwards, yet none has overcome the problem of human suffering. Many, in fact, have been a double-edged sword: splitting the atom produced both nuclear energy and the atomic bomb, and the invention of the automobile increased mobility but at the cost of CO_2 emissions. In the same way, disembodied minds may simply develop new forms of neurosis, and a network of discrete minds in cyberspace may turn out to resemble the multiple personalities of a schizophrenic. Faults can develop in even the most sophisticated AI: software and hardware upgrades will presumably be needed and may not always go according to plan. In sum, suffering may be endemic in life in a way that defies technological solution. While Buddhism may be sympathetic to the aims of Transhumanism in reducing suffering, therefore, it is unlikely to see the Singularity as an alternative to nirvana.

Glossary

adveṣa 'non-hatred' or benevolence

amoha 'non-delusion' or understanding

anātman the Buddhist doctrine of 'no self'

arāga 'non-attachment' or unselfishness

arhat a 'worthy one' or saint who has attained nirvana

ātman a permanent soul or self, the existence of which is denied in
Buddhist teachings

bodhisattva an 'enlightenment being', a follower of Mahāyāna
Buddhism

Brahma-vihāras 'sublime attitudes', a group of four states of mind
cultivated especially through meditation. They are: loving-kindness,
compassion, sympathetic joy, and equanimity

brahmin a member of the Hindu priestly caste

Buddha an 'awakened one', one who is fully enlightened and has
attained nirvana

Cakravartin a 'wheel turner', a mythical ideal ruler or righteous king

dāna generosity

Dharma natural law, Buddhist teachings

duḥkha suffering, unsatisfactoriness

dveṣa hatred

Jātakas stories of the Buddha's previous lives from the Khuddaka
Nikāya of the Pali canon

karma moral action and its consequences

karuṇā compassion

kleśa a negative disposition of character or vice

kṣānti patience

kuśala good, wholesome, virtuous

mantra a sound or formula having magic power

Māra the Buddhist 'Satan'

mizuko kuyō a memorial service following an abortion in Japan

moha delusion, ignorance

nirvana the goal of the Buddhist path; the state of perfect
enlightenment attained by Buddhas and *arhats*

pāṇa life, breath

paṇḍaka a 'queer person', or male suffering from a reproductive
disorder

pāpa evil deeds, bad karma; the opposite of *puṇya*

pāramitā one of the six 'perfections', or virtues, of a bodhisattva

prajñā knowledge, wisdom, insight

puṇya good deeds, merit, good karma; the opposite of *pāpa*

rāga desire, craving

samādhi meditative trance, concentration

saṃsāra cyclic existence

saṅgha the Buddhist order of monks and nuns

śīla morality, self-restraint

skandha one of the five components of human nature

sūtra/sutta a discourse of the Buddha

tripiṭaka the 'three baskets' of the Buddha's teachings, the Buddhist
canon

tṛṣṇā desire, craving

upāya-kauśalya 'Skilful Means', the doctrine that teachings and
practice can be adapted to circumstances

Vinaya Buddhist monastic law

References

Chapter 1: Buddhist morality

A translation of the *Dhammapada* is available online at <https://www.accesstoinsight.org/tipitaka/kn/dhp/dhp.intro.budd.html>; M. Cone and R. Gombrich (trans.), *The Perfect Generosity of Prince Vessantara* (Oxford: Clarendon Press, 1977); M. Tatz, *The Skill in Means (Upāyakauśalya) Sūtra* (New Delhi: Motilal Banarsidass, 1994); a translation of the *Lotus Sūtra* (from Tibetan) is available online at <http://read.84000.co/translation/toh113.html>.

Chapter 2: Ethics East and West

W. L. King, *In the Hope of Nibbana: The Ethics of Theravāda Buddhism* (La Salle, Ill.: Open Court, 1964); for a Kantian interpretation see P. Olson, *The Discipline of Freedom: A Kantian View of the Role of Moral Precepts in Zen Practice* (Albany, NY: State University of New York Press, 1993); for Buddhism as a form of negative utilitarianism see D. Breyer, 'The Cessation of Suffering and Buddhist Axiology', *Journal of Buddhist Ethics* 22 (2015), 533–60; the quote from Christopher Gowans is taken from C. Gowans, 'Buddhist Moral Thought and Western Moral Philosophy', in Jake H. Davis (ed.), *A Mirror is for Reflection: Understanding Buddhist Ethics* (New York: Oxford University Press, 2017), 53–69, 60; I. B. Horner (trans.), *Milinda's Questions: Milindapañha*, 2 vols (London: Pali Text Society, 1964); Lucius Annaeus Seneca, *Letters from a Stoic*, trans. Robin Campbell, reprint edn (Harmondsworth: Penguin Books, 1969); Marcus Aurelius and Diskin Clay, *Meditations*, ed. Martin Hammond

(London: Penguin Classics, 2015); Plato, *Euthyphro. Apology. Crito. Phaedo*, trans. Christopher Emlyn-Jones and William Preddy, bilingual edn (Cambridge, Mass., and London: Harvard University Press, 2001); C. Hallisey, 'Ethical Particularism in Theravāda Buddhism', *Journal of Buddhist Ethics* 3 (1996), 32–43, 37; W. D. Ross, *The Right and the Good* (Oxford: Oxford University Press, 2002); for Buddhist ethics as a form of 'character consequentialism' see C. Goodman, *Consequences of Compassion: An Interpretation and Defense of Buddhist Ethics* (Oxford and New York: Oxford University Press, 2009); A. Sen, *Human Rights and Asian Values* (New York: Carnegie Council on Ethics and International Affairs, 1997); the Dalai Lama is quoted in D. Keown, C. Prebish, and W. Husted, *Buddhism and Human Rights* (London: Curzon Press, 1998), xviii; S. B. King, *Being Benevolence: The Social Ethics of Engaged Buddhism* (Honolulu: University of Hawai'i Press, 2005), 139; P. A. Payutto is quoted in Martin Seeger, 'Theravāda Buddhism and Human Rights: Perspectives from Thai Buddhism', in Carmen Meinert and Hans-Bernd Zollner (eds), *Buddhist Approaches to Human Rights* (New Brunswick, NJ, and London: Transaction Publishers, 2010), 63–92, 82f.; H.-G. Gadamer, *Philosophical Hermeneutics*, trans. and ed. David E. Linge, 30th Anniversary edn (Berkeley: University of California Press, 2008), 7.

Chapter 3: Animals and the environment

L. White, Jr, 'The Historical Roots of Our Ecological Crisis', *Science* 155 (10 March 1967), 1203–7; Bodhi and Buddhaghosa (eds), *The Suttanipāta: An Ancient Collection of the Buddha's Discourses: Together with its Commentaries, Paramatthajotikā II and Excerpts from the Niddesa* (Sommerville, Mass.: Wisdom Publications, 2017); on the 'hermit strand' see L. Schmithausen, 'The Early Buddhist Tradition and Ethics', *Journal of Buddhist Ethics* 4 (1997), 1–74; the *Jīvaka Sutta* is available online at <https://www. accesstoinsight.org/tipitaka/an/an08/an08.026.than.html>; *A Buddhist Declaration on Climate Change* is available at <http:// gbccc.org>; P. Brancaccio, 'Angulimāla or the Taming of the Forest', *Philosophy East and West* 49, no. 1/4 (1999), 105–18, 116f.; I discuss the concept of 'karmic life' in D. Keown, *Buddhism and Bioethics* (London: Palgrave, 2001), 46–50; resources for

Buddhists seeking to minimize carbon pollution include
Ecobuddhism.org and OneEarthSangha.org.

Chapter 4: Sexuality and gender

Maurice Walshe (trans.), *Long Discourses of the Buddha:
Translation of the Dīgha-Nikāya*, 2nd rev. edn (Boston: Wisdom
Publications, 1996); for the *Abhidharmakośa-bhāṣya of
Vasubandhu*, see L. de la Vallée Poussin, P. Pradhan, and S. Jha,
The Abhidharmakośa of Vasubandhu, with the Commentary
(Patna: K. P. Jayaswal Research Institute, 1983); sGam Po Pa
and H. V. Guenther, *The Jewel Ornament of Liberation* (Boston:
Shambhala, 1986), 76; J. Powers, *Bull of a Man* (Cambridge,
Mass., and London: Harvard University Press, 2012); on
paṇḍakas, see P. Harvey, *An Introduction to Buddhist Ethics:
Foundations, Values and Issues* (Cambridge: Cambridge
University Press, 2000), 434; L. Zwilling is quoted in the same
volume (Harvey, *An Introduction to Buddhist Ethics*), 416;
J. I. Cabezon, *Sexuality in Classical South Asian Buddhism*
(Somerville, Mass.: Wisdom Publications, 2017); for the view
that *paṇḍakas* were simply a class of males who suffered from a
reproductive disorder see Paisarn Likhitpreechakul, 'Semen,
Viagra and *Paṇḍaka*: Ancient Endocrinology and Modern Day
Discrimination', *Journal of the Oxford Centre for Buddhist
Studies* 3 (2012), 91–127; documentation related to a report into
Rigpa by British law firm Lewis Silkin, with the response from
Rigpa, is available online <https://www.rigpa.org/independent-
investigation-report>; J. Gyatso, 'Sex', in D. Lopez (ed.), *Critical
Terms for the Study of Buddhism* (Chicago: University of
Chicago Press, 2005), 271–90; for the feminist view of Rita
Gross see R. M. Gross, *Buddhism After Patriarchy: A Feminist
History, Analysis, and Reconstruction of Buddhism* (Albany, NY:
State University of New York Press, 1992).

Chapter 5: War, violence, and terrorism

A history of recent wars is recorded by the Imperial War Museum
<https://www.iwm.org.uk/history/timeline-of-20th-and-21st-
century-wars>; K. R. Norman, *The Word of the Doctrine
(Dhammapada)*. Pali Text Society Translation Series No. 46

(Oxford: Pali Text Society, 2000); a public domain translation of the *Dhammapada Commentary* is available online at <http://www.aimwell.org/Dhammapada%20and%20Commentary.pdf>; an online facsimile of the six-volume translation of the *Jātaka* by E. B. Cowell is available at <https://archive.org/details/jatakaorstoriesofb01cowe>; various print and online editions of the *Mahāvaṃsa* are available, see <https://mahavamsa.org/>; S. Collins, *Nirvana and Other Buddhist Felicities: Utopias of the Pali Imaginaire* (Cambridge: Cambridge University Press, 1998), 420ff.; E. Ford, *Cold War Monks: Buddhism and America's Secret Strategy in Southeast Asia* (New Haven: Yale University Press, 2018); M. Jerryson, 'Buddhism, War, and Violence', in Daniel Cozort and James Mark Shields (eds),*The Oxford Handbook of Buddhist Ethics* (Oxford: Oxford University Press, 2018), 453–78, 454; Takuan quoted by P. Harvey, *An Introduction to Buddhist Ethics: Foundations, Values and Issues* (Cambridge: Cambridge University Press, 2000), 268; Harada Daiun Sōgaku quoted in B. D. A. Victoria, *Zen at War* (New York and Tokyo: Weatherhill, 1998), 137; Yasutani Haku'un quoted in D. Loy, 'Review of Zen War Stories', *Journal of Buddhist Ethics* 11 (2004), 67–73; 'In Infusing the Suicidal Japanese Military Spirit…', quoted in B. D. A. Victoria, *Zen War Stories* (London: Routledge Curzon, 2003), 144; S. Jenkins, 'The Range of the Bodhisattva: A Mahāyāna Sūtra', *Journal of Buddhist Ethics* 21 (2014), 429–41, 434; W. L. King, *Zen and the Way of the Sword: Arming the Samurai Psyche* (New York: Oxford University Press, 1993), 190–1; S. Raghavan, 'Politics of Sinhala Saṅgha: Venerable Walpola Rāhula', *Journal of the Oxford Centre for Buddhist Studies* 1 (2011), 114–33; Mipham, Jamgon, *The Just King: The Tibetan Buddhist Classic on Leading an Ethical Life*, trans. José Ignacio Cabezón (Boulder, Colo.: Snow Lion, 2017); the quotation from Aung San Suu Kyi is from an interview conducted by South Korea's *Buddhism* newspaper on the occasion of its 43rd Anniversary, 7 January 2003, report at <http://www.burmalibrary.org/TinKyi/archives/2003-01/msg00013.html>.

Chapter 6: Abortion

Bhikkhu Nyanamoli, *The Path of Purification* (Berkeley: Shambhala Publications, 1976); *The Lamp thoroughly Illuminating the Presentation of the Three Basic Bodies—Death*,

Intermediate State and Rebirth by Yang-jen-ga-way-lo-drö, trans.
Lati Rinbochay and J. Hopkins, *Death, Intermediate State and
Rebirth in Tibetan Buddhism* (London: Rider, 1979), 62; for an
example of a Buddhist pro-choice argument based on the idea of
evolving personhood see M. G. Barnhart, 'Buddhist Perspectives on
Abortion and Reproduction', in *The Oxford Handbook of Buddhist
Ethics* (Oxford: Oxford University Press, 2018), 592–610;
M. A. Warren, 'On the Moral and Legal Status of Abortion', *The
Monist*, 57, no. 1 (January 1973); 'Hymn to Jizo' from Masaharu
Anesaki, in J. A. MacCullagh et al. (eds), *The Mythology of All
Races* (New York: Cooper Square, 1964), vol. viii, 240; 'The
blessing of the child I had expected . . .' quoted in R. F. Young,
'Abortion, Grief, and Consolation: Prolegomena to a Christian
Response to Mizuko Kuyo', *Japan Christian Quarterly* (Tokyo) 55
(1989), 31–9; on abortion in Japan see M. Kato, 'Abortion and the
Pill: Abortion still Key Birth Control', *The Japan Times*, 20
October 2009; J. Wilson, *Mourning the Unborn Dead: A Buddhist
Ritual Comes to America* (New York and Oxford: Oxford
University Press, 2009).

Chapter 7: Suicide and euthanasia

D. Halberstam, *The Making of a Quagmire* (New York: Random
House, 1965), 128; 'Before closing my eyes to go to Buddha . . .'
quoted in Charles A. Joiner, 'South Vietnam's Buddhist Crisis:
Organization for Charity, Dissidence, and Unity', *Asian Survey* 4,
no. 7 (1964), 915–28, 918; Thich Nhat Hanh, *Vietnam: The Lotus
in a Sea of Fire* (London: SCM Press, 1967); for translations of the
Brahmajāla Sūtra see S. Shigeru, *The Very Mahayana Buddhist
Ethics: Introduction and Translation of the 'Fan-Wang-Ching'*
(Tokyo: Chuo University Press, 2005), or <http://www.ymba.org/
books/brahma-net-sutra-moral-code-bodhisattva/brahma-net-
sutra>; the Dalai Lama quoted in C. Campbell, 'The Dalai Lama
Has Been the Face of Buddhism for 60 Years: China Wants to
Change That', *Time*, 7 March 2019 <http://time.com/longform/
dalai-lama-60-year-exile/>; J. Benn, 'Where Text Meets Flesh:
Burning the Body as an "Apocryphal Practice" in Chinese
Buddhism', *History of Religions* 37, no. 4 (May 1998), 295–322;
D. Keown, 'Buddhism and Suicide: The Case of Channa', *Journal of
Buddhist Ethics*, 3 (1996), 8–31; statistics on self-immolation by
Tibetans are available from the International Campaign for Tibet:

<http://www.savetibet.org/resources/fact-sheets/self-immolations-by-tibetans/>; the most recent 'Declaration on Euthanasia and Physician-Assisted Suicide' by the World Medical Association dated 27 October 2019 can be found at <https://www.wma.net/policies-post/declaration-on-euthanasia-and-physician-assisted-suicide/>.

Chapter 8: Clones, cyborgs, and singularities

Professor Yong Moon, 'Buddhism at One with Stem Cell Research', *ABC Science Online*, <http://www.abc.net.au/science/news/stories/s1046974.htm>, 18 February 2004; G. E. Pence, *Who's Afraid of Human Cloning?* (Lanham, Md: Rowman and Littlefield, 1998), 1; Buddhaghosa's comments on twins can be found at *Visuddhimagga* 575 and DA.ii.509; 'The Proceedings of the First Conference on Gene Editing' are available at <http://nationalacad-emies.org/gene-editing/Gene-Edit-Summit/index.htm>; see also the commentary in *Nature* by leading scientists calling for a moratorium on hereditable genome editing, <https://www.nature.com/articles/d41586-019-00726-5>; 'Transhumanism is a class of philosophies...' from <https://humanityplus.org/philosophy/>; J. J. Hughes, 'Using Neurotechnologies to Develop Virtues: A Buddhist Approach to Cognitive Enhancement', *Accountability in Research: Policies and Quality Assurance* 20, no. 1 (1 January 2013), 27–41, 10; for a sceptical view of virtue enhancement see N. Agar, 'Moral Bioenhancement is Dangerous', *Journal of Medical Ethics* 41, no. 4 (1 April 2015), 343–5; J. J. Hughes, 'Cyborg Buddha', *Tricycle* (Summer 2010); the Cyborg Buddha Project has a website at <https://ieet.org/index.php/IEET2/cyborgbuddha>; B. Russell, *The Conquest of Happiness* (London: Routledge, 2015), 37; J. Habermas, *Future of Human Nature* (Cambridge: Polity Press, 2003); F. Fukuyama, 'Transhumanism', *Foreign Policy* (blog) <https://foreignpolicy.com/2009/10/23/transhumanism/>.

Further reading

General resources

Readers will find further information on many of the topics covered in this introduction in P. Harvey, *An Introduction to Buddhist Ethics: Foundations, Values and Issues* (Cambridge: Cambridge University Press, 2000). Articles on a range of specific issues and topics are also available in Daniel Cozort and James Mark Shields (eds), *The Oxford Handbook of Buddhist Ethics* (Oxford: Oxford University Press, 2018). The *Journal of Buddhist Ethics* has a large selection of articles freely available online at <https://blogs.dickinson.edu/buddhistethics/>.

Chapter 1: Buddhist morality

P. Groner, 'The Bodhisattva Precepts', in *The Oxford Handbook of Buddhist Ethics* (Oxford: Oxford University Press, 2018), 29–50; P. Harvey, *An Introduction to Buddhist Ethics: Foundations, Values and Issues* (Cambridge: Cambridge University Press, 2000), chapters 1–3; P. Harvey, 'Karma', in *The Oxford Handbook of Buddhist Ethics* (Oxford: Oxford University Press, 2018), 7–28; D. Keown, *Buddhism: A Very Short Introduction*, 2nd edn (Oxford: Oxford University Press, 2013); C. S. Prebish, 'The Vinaya', in *The Oxford Handbook of Buddhist Ethics* (Oxford: Oxford University Press, 2018), 96–115; M. Pye, *Skilful Means: A Concept in Mahāyāna Buddhism* (London: Duckworth, 1978); H. Saddhatissa, *Buddhist Ethics* (Boston: Wisdom, 1997);

J. Whitaker and Douglass Smith, 'Ethics, Meditation, and Wisdom', in *The Oxford Handbook of Buddhist Ethics* (Oxford: Oxford University Press, 2018), 51–73; M. Wijayaratana, *Buddhist Monastic Life* (Cambridge: Cambridge University Press, 1990).

Chapter 2: Ethics East and West

S. Blackburn, *Ethics: A Very Short Introduction* (Oxford: Oxford University Press, 2003); D. J. Fasching and D. Dechant (eds), *Comparative Religious Ethics: A Narrative Approach* (Oxford: Blackwell, 2001); C. Goodman, *Consequences of Compassion: An Interpretation and Defense of Buddhist Ethics* (Oxford and New York: Oxford University Press, 2009); C. Gowans, *Buddhist Moral Philosophy: An Introduction* (New York: Taylor and Francis, 2015); R. Hindery, *Comparative Ethics in Hindu and Buddhist Traditions* (Delhi: Motilal Banarsidas, 1978); W. B. Irvine, *A Guide to the Good Life: The Ancient Art of Stoic Joy* (Oxford and New York: Oxford University Press, 2008); D. Keown, 'Human Rights', in *The Oxford Handbook of Buddhist Ethics*, ed. Daniel Cozort and James Mark Shields (Oxford: Oxford University Press, 2018), 531–51; D. Keown, C. Prebish, and W. Husted, *Buddhism and Human Rights* (London: Curzon Press, 1998); D. Keown, *The Nature of Buddhist Ethics* (Basingstoke: Palgrave, 2001); S. B. King, *Being Benevolence: The Social Ethics of Engaged Buddhism* (Honolulu: University of Hawai'i Press, 2005); S. B. King, 'Buddhism and Human Rights', in *Religion and Human Rights: An Introduction*, ed. John Witte Jr and M. Christian Green (Oxford and New York: Oxford University Press, 2012), 103–18; D. Little and S. B. Twiss, *Comparative Religious Ethics* (San Francisco: Harper and Row, 1978); C. Meinert and Hans-Bernd Zollner, *Buddhist Approaches to Human Rights* (New Brunswick, NJ, and London: Transaction Publishers, 2010); C. Queen, *Engaged Buddhism in the West* (Boston: Wisdom, 2000); C. Queen, Charles Prebish, and Damien Keown (eds), *Action Dharma: New Studies in Engaged Buddhism* (London: Routledge Curzon, 2003); S. Meynard Vasen, 'Buddhist Ethics Compared to Western Ethics', in *The Oxford Handbook of Buddhist Ethics* (Oxford: Oxford University Press, 2018), 317–34; H. Widdows, 'Is Global Ethics Moral Neo-Colonialism? An Investigation of the

Issue in the Context of Bioethics', *Bioethics* 21, no. 6 (1 July 2007), 305–15.

Chapter 3: Animals and the environment

A. H. Badiner, *Dharma Gaia*: *A Harvest of Essays in Buddhism and Ecology* (Berkeley: Parallax Press, 1990); G. Barstow, *Food of Sinful Demons: Meat, Vegetarianism, and the Limits of Buddhism in Tibet* (New York: Columbia University Press, 2019); Bodhipaksa, *Vegetarianism* (Birmingham: Windhorse, 1999); S. Dhammika, *Nature and the Environment in Early Buddhism* (Singapore: Buddha Dhamma Mandala Society, 2015); I. Harris, 'Buddhism and Ecology', in Damien Keown (ed.), *Contemporary Buddhist Ethics* (Richmond: Curzon Press, 2000), 113–35; P. Harvey, *An Introduction to Buddhist Ethics: Foundations, Values and Issues* (Cambridge: Cambridge University Press, 2000), chapter 4; A. Heirman, 'How to Deal with Dangerous and Annoying Animals: A Vinaya Perspective', *Religions* 10, no. 2 (2019), 113; S. P. James, *Zen Buddhism and Environmental Ethics* (Aldershot: Ashgate, 2003); S. Kaza and K. Kraft, *Dharma Rain: Sources of Buddhist Environmentalism* (Boston: Shambhala Publications, 2000); S. Kaza, 'Buddhist Environmental Ethics: An Emergent and Contextual Approach', in *The Oxford Handbook of Buddhist Ethics* (Oxford: Oxford University Press, 2018), 432–52; J. Macy, *World as Lover, World as Self* (Berkeley: Parallax Press, 1991); R. Ohnuma, *Unfortunate Destiny: Animals in the Indian Buddhist Imagination* (New York: Oxford University Press, 2017); K. Sandell (ed.), *Buddhist Perspectives on the Ecocrisis* (Kandy: Buddhist Publication Society, 1987); L. Schmithausen, 'The Early Buddhist Tradition and Ethics', *Journal of Buddhist Ethics* 4 (1997), 1–74; L. Schmithausen, 'Buddhism and the Ethics of Nature: Some Remarks', *The Eastern Buddhist*, New Series 32 (2000), 26–78; P. de Silva, *Environmental Philosophy and Ethics in Buddhism* (New York: St Martin's Press, 1998); M. E. Tucker and D. R. Williams, *Buddhism and Ecology*: *The Interconnection of Dharma and Deeds* (Cambridge, Mass.: Harvard University Press, 1997); P. Waldau, *The Specter of Speciesism*: *Buddhist and Christian Views of Animals* (New York: Oxford University Press, 2002); T. Page, *Buddhism and Animals* (London: Ukavis, 1999); J. Stewart, *Vegetarianism and Animal Ethics in Contemporary Buddhism* (Routledge, 2018).

J. I. Cabezón, *Buddhism, Sexuality, and Gender* (Albany, NY: State University of New York Press, 1992); J. I. Cabezón, *Sexuality in Classical South Asian Buddhism* (Somerville, Mass.: Wisdom Publications, 2017); S. Collins, 'Remarks on the Third Precept: Adultery and Prostitution in Pali Texts', *Journal of the Pali Text Society* 29 (2007), 263–84; U. Das, 'Women, Marriage, and Merit-Making in Early Buddhism', *Journal of Dharma Studies* 1, no. 1 (1 October 2018), 129–45; B. Faure, *The Red Thread: Buddhist Approaches to Sexuality* (Princeton: Princeton University Press, 1998); B. Faure, *The Power of Denial: Buddhism, Purity, and Gender* (Princeton: Princeton University Press, 2003); C. Gamage, *Buddhism and Sensuality: As Recorded in the Theravāda Canon* (Evanston, Ill.: Northwestern University, 1998); A. Gleig, 'Queering Buddhism or Buddhist De-Queering?', *Theology & Sexuality* 18, no. 3 (1 January 2012), 198–214; R. M. Gross, *Buddhism After Patriarchy: A Feminist History, Analysis, and Reconstruction of Buddhism* (Albany, NY: State University of New York Press, 1992); P. Harvey, *An Introduction to Buddhist Ethics: Foundations, Values and Issues* (Cambridge: Cambridge University Press, 2000), chapters 9–10; W. A. LaFleur, 'Sex, Rhetoric, and Ontology: Fecundism as an Ethical Problem', in S. Ellingson and M. C. Green (eds), *Religion and Sexuality in Cross-Cultural Perspective* (London: Routledge, 2003), 51–82; A. P. Langenberg, 'Buddhism and Sexuality', in *The Oxford Handbook of Buddhist Ethics* (Oxford: Oxford University Press, 2018), 567–91; L. P. N. Perera, *Sexuality in Ancient India: A Study Based on the Pali Vinayapitaka* (Kelaniya, Sri Lanka: University of Kelaniya, 1993); J. Powers, *Bull of a Man* (Cambridge, Mass., and London: Harvard University Press, 2012); S. Smith, Sally Munt, and Andrew Yip, *Cosmopolitan Dharma: Race, Sexuality, and Gender in British Buddhism* (Leiden and Boston: Brill, 2016); J. Stevens, *Lust for Enlightenment: Buddhism and Sex* (Boston: Shambhala, 1990); J. Whitaker, 'A Storm is Coming: Tibetan Buddhism in the West', *Patheos* American Buddhist Perspectives (blog), 15 November 2017. <https://www.patheos.com/blogs/americanbuddhist/2017/11/a-storm-is-coming-tibetan-buddhism-in-the-west.html>.

Chapter 5: War, violence, and terrorism

A. Abeysekara, *Colors of the Robe* (Columbia, SC: University of South Carolina Press, 2008); T. J. Bartholomeusz, *In Defence of Dharma*: *Just-war Ideology in Buddhist Sri Lanka* (London: Routledge Curzon, 2002); A. J. Coates, *The Ethics of War*, 2nd edn (Manchester: Manchester University Press, 2016); E. J. Harris, 'Buddhism and the Justification of War: A Case Study from Sri Lanka', in P. Robinson (ed.), *Just War in Comparative Perspective* (Aldershot: Ashgate, 2003), 93–106; I. Harris, *Buddhism and Politics in Twentieth-Century Asia* (London: Continuum, 2001); P. Harvey, *An Introduction to Buddhist Ethics*: *Foundations, Values and Issues* (Cambridge: Cambridge University Press, 2000), chapter 6; P. D. Hershock, 'From Vulnerability to Virtuosity: Buddhist Reflections on Responding to Terrorism and Tragedy', *Journal of Buddhist Ethics* 10 (2003), 21–38; E. Ford, *Cold War Monks: Buddhism and America's Secret Strategy in Southeast Asia* (New Haven: Yale University Press, 2018); M. Jerryson, 'Buddhism, War, and Violence', in Daniel Cozort and James Mark Shields (eds), *The Oxford Handbook of Buddhist Ethics* (Oxford: Oxford University Press, 2018), 453–78; K. Kraft, *Inner Peace, World Peace*: *Essays on Buddhism and Nonviolence* (Albany, NY: State University of New York Press, 1992); P. Lehr, *Militant Buddhism: The Rise of Religious Violence in Sri Lanka, Myanmar and Thailand* (New York: Palgrave Macmillan, 2018); G. D. Paige and S. Gilliatt, *Buddhism and Non-Violent Global Problem-Solving* (Honolulu: Center for Global Nonviolence Planning Project, Spark M. Matsunaga Institute for Peace, University of Hawaii Press, 1991); L. Schmithausen, 'Aspects of the Buddhist Attitude Towards War', in Jan E. M. Houben and Karel R. Van Kooij (eds), *Violence Denied: Violence, Non-Violence and the Rationalization of Violence in South Asian Cultural History* (Leiden: Brill, 1999), 45–67; U. Tahtinen, *Non-Violent Theories of Punishment: Indian and Western* (Delhi: Motilal Banarsidass, 1983); B. D. A. Victoria, *Zen at War* (New York and Tokyo: Weatherhill, 1997); B. D. A. Victoria, *Zen War Stories* (London: Routledge Curzon, 2003); M. J. Walton, *Buddhism and the Political: Organisation and Participation in the Theravāda Moral Universe* (New York: C. Hurst & Co. Publishers Ltd, 2020).

Chapter 6: Abortion

A comprehensive annotated bibliography can be found in the author's article 'Buddhism and Abortion' in the online *Oxford Bibliographies* series; M. G. Barnhart, 'Buddhist Perspectives on Abortion and Reproduction', in Daniel Cozort and James Mark Shields (eds), *The Oxford Handbook of Buddhist Ethics* (Oxford: Oxford University Press, 2018), 592–610; R. Florida, 'Buddhism and Abortion', in D. Keown (ed.), *Contemporary Buddhist Ethics* (Richmond: Curzon Press, 2000); H. Glassman, *The Face of Jizō: Image and Cult in Medieval Japanese Buddhism* (Honolulu: University of Hawai'i Press, 2012); H. Hardacre, *Marketing the Menacing Fetus in Japan* (Berkeley: University of California Press, 1997); P. Harvey, *An Introduction to Buddhist Ethics: Foundations, Values and Issues* (Cambridge: Cambridge University Press, 2000), chapter 8; D. Keown, *Buddhism and Abortion* (London/Honolulu: Macmillan/University of Hawaii Press, 1999); D. Keown, *Buddhism and Bioethics* (London: Palgrave, 2001), 65–138; W. A. LaFleur, *Liquid Life: Abortion and Buddhism in Japan* (Princeton: Princeton University Press, 1992); A. Whittaker, *Abortion, Sin and the State in Thailand* (London: RoutledgeCurzon, 2004); J. Wilson, *Mourning the Unborn Dead: A Buddhist Ritual Comes to America* (New York and Oxford: Oxford University Press, 2009).

Chapter 7: Suicide and euthanasia

D. Keown, 'Euthanasia', in D. Cozort and J. M. Shields (eds), *The Oxford Handbook of Buddhist Ethics* (Oxford and New York: Oxford University Press, 2018), 611–29; M. Kovan, 'Being and its Other: Suicide in Buddhist Ethics', in *The Oxford Handbook of Buddhist Ethics* (Oxford: Oxford University Press, 2018), 630–49; C. B. Becker, 'Buddhist Views of Suicide and Euthanasia', *Philosophy East and West* 40 (1990), 543–56; R. Florida, 'Buddhist Approaches to Euthanasia', *Studies in Religion* [*Sciences religieuses*] 22 (1993), 35–47; P. Harvey, *An Introduction to Buddhist Ethics: Foundations, Values and Issues* (Cambridge: Cambridge University Press, 2000), chapter 7; D. Keown and J. Keown, 'Karma, Killing and Caring: Buddhist and Christian Perspectives on Euthanasia', *Journal of Medical Ethics* 21 (1995), 265–9; R. W. Perrett, 'Buddhism, Euthanasia and the Sanctity of Life', *Journal of*

Medical Ethics 22 (1996), 309–13; P. Ratanakul, 'To Save or Let Go: Thai Buddhist Perspectives on Euthanasia', in D. Keown (ed.), *Contemporary Buddhist Ethics* (Richmond: Curzon Press, 2000), 169–82; A. Terrone, 'Burning for a Cause: Self-Immolations, Human Security, and the Violence of Nonviolence in Tibet', *Journal of Buddhist Ethics* 25 (2018), 465–529; J. Yu, 'Reflections on Self-Immolation in Chinese Buddhist and Daoist Traditions', in Margo Kitts (ed.), *Martyrdom, Self-Sacrifice, and Self-Immolation: Religious Perspectives on Suicide* (New York: Oxford University Press, 2018), 264–79.

Chapter 8: Clones, cyborgs, and singularities

M. G. Barnhart, 'Nature, Nurture, and No-Self: Bioengineering and Buddhist Values', *Journal of Buddhist Ethics* 7 (2000), 126–44; A. Buben, 'Personal Immortality in Transhumanism and Ancient Indian Philosophy', *Philosophy East and West* (Early Release Article, 2019 <https://doi.org/doi:10.1353/pew.0.0131>); B. Huimin, 'Buddhist Bioethics: The Case of Human Cloning and Embryo Stem Cell Research' (in Chinese), *Chung-Hwa Buddhist Journal* 15 (2002), 457–70; J. J. Hughes, 'Buddhism and our Posthuman Future', *Sophia* (26 October 2018) <https://doi.org/10.1007/s11841-018-0669-2>; A. Huxley, 'The Pali Buddhist Approach to Human Cloning', in S. Voneki and Rüdiger Wolfrum (eds), *Human Dignity and Human Cloning* (Leiden: Springer, 2004), 13–22; M. LaTorra, 'What is Buddhist Transhumanism?', *Theology and Science* 13, no. 2 (3 April 2015), 219–29; J. Rifkin, *The Biotech Century* (London: Phoenix, 1999); J. Schlieter, 'Some Observations on Buddhist Thoughts on Human Cloning', in H. Roetz, *Cross-Cultural Issues in Bioethics—The Example of Human Cloning* (Amsterdam: Rodopi, 2006), 179–202; P. Ratanakul, 'Human Cloning: Thai Buddhist Perspectives', in H. Roetz (ed.), *Cross-Cultural Issues in Bioethics: The Example of Human Cloning* (Amsterdam: Rodopi, 2006), 203–14; J. Tham, Chris Durante, and Alberto García Gómez (eds), *Interreligious Perspectives on Mind, Genes and the Self: Emerging Technologies and Human Identity* (Abingdon, Oxon. and New York: Routledge, 2018).

Index

For the benefit of digital users, indexed terms that span two pages (e.g., 52–53) may, on occasion, appear on only one of those pages.

A

Abhidharmakośa 53, 62
abortion 18, 27, 77–92, 99–100
adultery 52–4
ahimsā 9–11, 19–20, 41, 54, 70, 72, 77, 102–3
AI (artificial intelligence) 117–18, 123–4
Ajātasattu 63–4
Ānanda 50
antinomianism 16
Aquinas, St Thomas 69
arhat 13, 64–5, 98–9
Aristotle 19
Aśoka 32
ātman 56, 62
Aung San Suu Kyi 74–5
autonomy 81, 103–4, 118, 123
Avalokiteśvara 14, 59

B

Benn, James 97
Bentham, Jeremy 18–19

bodhisattva 12–15, 41, 59, 87–8, 95–6, 116, 122
Brahmajāla Sūtra 97–8
Brahma-vihāras 13, 33–4
Buddha 1–3, 5–6, 8, 10–11, 14–15, 20, 33–8, 40–3, 50–1, 54–6, 62, 77–8, 80, 97–101, 103–4, 106, 109–11
Buddhaghosa 40–1, 54–6, 78, 82–4, 103–5, 109
Buddhist Hospice Trust 104

C

Cakravartin 63, 70
celibacy 15–16, 48, 60
Channa 99
Christianity 7, 31–2, 48, 50–1
climate change 46
cloning 107–9, 113
Collins, Steven 63–4
compassion (*karuṇā*) 1, 9–10, 13–16, 21, 33–4, 42–6, 54, 63, 66–7, 71–2, 74–6, 91, 102–3, 119–20

CRISPR 112–13
cryonics 114–15
cyborg 117, 119–20

D

Dalai Lama 28, 57–8, 68, 70, 96–7,
    115, 119
dāna (generosity) 9, 11–13
deep ecology 45
delusion (*moha*) 5–6, 20, 62,
    105, 113
deontology 18, 21
Dharma 1–4, 6–8, 11, 57–8,
    63–4, 98
DNA 107–11, 113
Dolly (the sheep) 107–8
duḥkha 20, 49
Duṭṭhagāmaṇi 64–5
duty 49

E

ecofeminism 45
ecology 35–6, 40–1, 44–8
Eightfold Path 3–4, 13, 20,
    33, 54
Eight Precepts 8
embryo 78, 82–4
embryology 77–9
embryonic Buddha 33–4
emptiness (*śūnyatā*) 66
enlightenment (*bodhi*) 24, 35, 37,
    44–5, 109–11, 119, 122–3
ethics
    applied normative 31–2
    descriptive 17–18
    normative 17–18, 23–4
    three branches of 17–18
eugenics 113
euthanasia 27, 96, 99–104, 106
    active 101–2
    passive 101–2
    voluntary 101
Euthyphro 24

F

First precept 10, 32, 39–40, 46, 62,
    77, 79–80, 83–4
Five Precepts 7–8, 19–20
Ford, Eugene 65–6
Four Noble Truths 3
Fukuyama, Francis 123

G

Gadamer, Hans-Georg 28–9
gandharva 77–8, 111
gene editing 29, 43–4, 107, 112–13
Genesis, Book of 49
germ line therapy 112–13
Golden Rule 11, 54
Gowans, Christopher 24
greed (*rāga*) 5–6, 20, 34–5, 43,
    62, 113
Gross, Rita 58–60
Gyatso, Janet 57–8

H

Halberstam, David 93
Hallisey, Charles 20–1
hara kiri 97–8
Harada Daiun Sōgaku 66–7
Harvey, Peter 56
hatred (*dveṣa*) 5–6, 20, 62, 64,
    73, 113
Heart Sūtra 88–9
He Jiankui, Dr 112
'hermit strand' 37
Hīnayāna 26–7
homosexuality 54–6, 58–9
Hughes, James 119–21, 123
Hwang Woo-Suk 113

I

Ikeda, Daisetsu 68
Indra's net 31–2, 45
intention (*cetanā*) 5–6, 101–2

intercourse 16, 52–4, 56–60, 77–8
in-vitro fertilization (IVF) 111

J

Jainism 10
Japan 51, 64, 66–8, 75–6, 86–7, 89–91, 97–8
Jerryson, Michael 64, 75–6
Jizō Bosatsu 87–90
Jōdō Shinshū 91
jus ad bellum 69–70, 73
jus in bello 69–70, 73

K

Kant, Immanuel 18, 81
karma 1–7, 19–21, 24–5, 34–6, 46, 59, 62, 85–6, 89–91, 103–4, 106–8, 111
karmic life 39–40
kaṭhina 11
King, Winston 17
Kittivuḍḍho 65–6
kleśa 9
Kṣitigarbha 87–8
Kurzweil, Ray 114, 117
kuśala 5–6

L

Langenberg, Amy 49
Laṅkāvatāra Sūtra 43
La Torra, Michael 119–20
Locke, John 81
Lopez, Donald 108
Lotus Sūtra 14–15

M

Mahāyāna 7–8, 10, 12–15, 22, 26–7, 33–4, 41, 43, 66, 84, 98
Māra 51, 65–6
Marcus Aurelius 25

marriage 49, 51–4, 58, 74
masturbation 56–7
meditation (*samādhi*) 3–4, 13, 99–100, 119
merit (*puṇya*) 6–7, 11, 31–2, 35–6, 65–6, 75–6
merit transference 7
metaethics 17–18, 23–4
mettā 54
Milinda's Questions 24
Mill, John Stuart 18–19
Mipham 70–2, 76
mizuko kuyō 86–91
monogamy 52
moxibustion 81

N

nāmā-rūpa 78, 82–3
Nipponzan Myōhōji 68
nirvana 3, 12, 19–20, 25, 44–5, 49–50, 106–7, 123–4

P

pacifism 68, 75–6
paṇḍakas 56
pāpa 6
pārājika 37–8, 79–80, 99–104
Particularism 20–1
patience (*kṣānti*) 13, 62
Peace Pagodas 68
Pence, Gregory E. 108
Perfectionism 21–2
Perfections (*pāramitā*) 12–13
persistent vegetative state (PVS) 105
personhood 81–3
Phra Pisarn Thammapatee 57
physician assisted suicide 102, 106
plants 33, 35–6, 44–5, 47
poṣadha 8–9
Powers, John 51
prāṇa 32, 79
Prātimokṣa 8–9, 35

Prātimokṣa-sūtra 8–9
precepts 1, 6–10, 12, 15–20, 23–4,
    35, 41, 52–4
procreation 49, 60
Pure Land 14, 66–7

R

realms of rebirth 87
refuge (going for) 7–8
'releasing life' (*fang sheng*)
    31–2, 41
rights 17, 26–8, 32, 37–8, 41, 57, 65,
    75, 91–2, 118, 123
Risshō Kōsei-kai 68
roots (good and bad) 5–6
Ross, W. D. 20–1

S

St Augustine 69
St Paul 51
Śākya 63
saṃsāra 1–3, 38, 44–5, 49, 51
samurai 97–8
San Francisco Zen Center 104
saṅgha 6, 8–9, 11, 59, 63–5, 86,
Śāriputra 99
Schmithausen, Lambert 37
Sen, Amartya 28
Seneca 25
seppuku 97–8, 101
sex abuse scandals 55
śila (moral conduct) 4, 7, 12
Singularity 117, 123–4
skandhas 22, 82
skilful means (*upaya-kauśalya*)
    14–15, 21, 41, 66
Skill-in-Means Sūtra (*Upāya-
    kauśalya-sūtra*) 15–16
Socrates 24
Sōka Gakkai 68
śramaṇas 8
Sri Lanka 64–5, 75, 85

Stoicism 24–5
suicide 93–102, 106
    altruistic 96, 106
    religious 96
Śūramgamasamādhi Sūtra 97

T

Takuan Sōhō Zenji 66
Tantra 16
tatari 89–91
Ten Good Paths of Action 8
Ten Precepts 8
terrorism 72–6
Thailand 38, 59, 64–6, 84–5
Theravāda 11–12, 17, 84
Thich Nhat Hanh 26–7, 73, 95
Thich Quang Duc 93–4,
    96–7, 106
Tibet 28, 48, 53, 64, 68, 70
transgenderism 59
Transhumanism 116, 119, 123–4

U

Upāya-kauśalya-sūtra see
    Skill-in-Means Sūtra
utilitarianism 18–21, 23

V

Vajrayāna 16, 26–7
Vasubandhu 62
vegetarianism 10, 42–4
Vessantara 12
Victoria, Brian 66–7, 75
Vinaya 8–9, 44, 48–9, 51–2,
    56, 79–80, 83–4, 99–100,
    102–3
virtue ethics 18–22
virtues 1, 9, 11–13, 20, 22–5, 35,
    45–6, 54, 120–1, 123
vivisection 43–4
voluntary death 96

W

war 11, 18, 61–2, 64–7, 71–2, 75–6
  holy 64–5
  just 68–70, 73
Warren, Mary Anne 81–2
wheel of life (*bhavacakra*) 38–9
White, Lynn 31
wisdom (*prajñā*) 3–4, 13, 21–2, 25,
  45–6, 55, 110–11, 120, 122
women 45, 48–56, 58–60, 85–92

Y

Yasutani Haku'un 66–7
Yongming Yanshou 97

Z

Zen 1, 55, 66–8, 75, 104
Zeno (of Citium) 25
Zwilling, Leonard 56

CHRISTIAN ETHICS
A Very Short Introduction
D. Stephen Long

This *Very Short Introduction* to Christian ethics introduces the topic by examining its sources and historical basis. D. Stephen Long presents a discussion of the relationship between Christian ethics, modern, and postmodern ethics, and explores practical issues including sex, money, and power. Long recognises the inherent difficulties in bringing together 'Christian' and 'ethics' but argues that this is an important task for both the Christian faith and for ethics. Arguing that Christian ethics are not a precise science, but the cultivation of practical wisdom from a range of sources, Long also discusses some of the failures of the Christian tradition, including the crusades, the conquest, slavery, inquisitions, and the Galileo affair.

www.oup.com/vsi

EXISTENTIALISM
A Very Short Introduction
Thomas Flynn

Existentialism was one of the leading philosophical movements of the twentieth century. Focusing on its seven leading figures, Sartre, Nietzsche, Heidegger, Kierkegaard, de Beauvoir, Merleau-Ponty and Camus, this *Very Short Introduction* provides a clear account of the key themes of the movement which emphasized individuality, free will, and personal responsibility in the modern world. Drawing in the movement's varied relationships with the arts, humanism, and politics, this book clarifies the philosophy and original meaning of 'existentialism' - which has tended to be obscured by misappropriation. Placing it in its historical context, Thomas Flynn also highlights how existentialism is still relevant to us today.

www.oup.com/vsi

CONSCIENCE
A Very Short Introduction
Paul Strohm

In the West conscience has been relied upon for two thousand years as a judgement that distinguishes right from wrong. It has effortlessly moved through every period division and timeline between the ancient, medieval, and modern. The Romans identified it, the early Christians appropriated it, and Reformation Protestants and loyal Catholics relied upon its advice and admonition. Today it is embraced with equal conviction by non-religious and religious alike. Considering its deep historical roots and exploring what it has meant to successive generations, Paul Strohm highlights why this particularly European concept deserves its reputation as 'one of the prouder Western contributions to human rights and human dignity throughout the world.

www.oup.com/vsi

GERMAN PHILOSOPHY
A Very Short Introduction
Andrew Bowie

German Philosophy: A Very Short Introduction discusses the idea that German philosophy forms one of the most revealing responses to the problems of 'modernity'. The rise of the modern natural sciences and the related decline of religion raises a series of questions, which recur throughout German philosophy, concerning the relationships between knowledge and faith, reason and emotion, and scientific, ethical, and artistic ways of seeing the world. There are also many significant philosophers who are generally neglected in most existing English-language treatments of German philosophy, which tend to concentrate on the canonical figures. This *Very Short Introduction* will include reference to these thinkers and suggests how they can be used to question more familiar German philosophical thought.

www.oup.com/vsi

HUMAN RIGHTS
A Very Short Introduction
Andrew Clapham

An appeal to human rights in the face of injustice can be a heartfelt and morally justified demand for some, while for others it remains merely an empty slogan. Taking an international perspective and focusing on highly topical issues such as torture, arbitrary detention, privacy, health and discrimination, this *Very Short Introduction* will help readers to understand for themselves the controversies and complexities behind this vitally relevant issue. Looking at the philosophical justification for rights, the historical origins of human rights and how they are formed in law, Andrew Clapham explains what our human rights actually are, what they might be, and where the human rights movement is heading.

www.oup.com/vsi